THE HISTORY
OF
CHESHAM UNITED
FOOTBALL CLUB

Frontispiece

*Chesham Footballers and Cricketers at The Meadow
with the famous W.G. Grace around the turn of the Century*

THE HISTORY
OF
CHESHAM UNITED
FOOTBALL CLUB

by
Peter Gibbins

This book is dedicated to Anita and Jack.
Without their patience, co-operation and understanding,
it would never have been possible.

Published by Peter Gibbins
Chartridge, Chesham, Bucks.
ISBN No. 0 9532691 0 8

Typography, Layout and Design by Castle Printers, East Wittering, West Sussex.
Printed and Bound in Great Britain by Biddles Ltd., Guildford, Surrey.

Copies limited to 1000

.... of 1000

CONTENTS

INTRODUCTION

Chesham United Football Club's history is a fascinating story, mixing failure and achievement in equal measure. I've been at the bottom and top of the pile at Chesham. My experiences of sixteen years exposure to all aspects of the Club from being a player through to being a director have left me with wonderful memories.

But the history of our family's connection with the Club goes back some sixty years to the days when Granddad Bill Page first turned out for Chesham United. Things were quite different in those days, when all the players were local lads and they wore their hearts on the sleeves. There was a real feeling of pride in playing for the Town. The introduction of professional players soon put an end to players from the Town, particularly as improved transport enabled players to travel further afield.

The next family member to play for the Club was uncle Pete Wells, who donned the claret and blue during in the 1950's and 1960's. He eventually retired from playing football in 1980 aged 50 odd. Then came the Club's current President, my father-in-law Bill Wells, who graced the hallowed turf from 1956 for several seasons until a farm accident caused a sudden end to his playing career. Little did he know that coming seasons would bring elation and despair.

After a spell in the army doing national service, football beckoned again, with an invitation to join the board at Tring, where two of his brothers played. Bill eventually became chairman of the Tring board. Also on Tring's board was Geoff Smith, who became Vice-Chairman of Watford FC. Some years later Bill was invited to join the romantic Vicarage Road club, then under Elton John's chairmanship. After several years looking after the ground and Junior Hornets, Bill left and joined Aylesbury as chairman and steered them to their new ground at Watermeet.

Then an opportunity arose at Chesham and he was able to go back to his first love, returning to the Meadow as a director and eventually President of the Club.

The most well known of our family members to play at Chesham was uncle Dennis Wells, "the man with the hands." Dennis was the local lad drafted into the lime light at the eleventh hour and who saved the day. The regular keeper, Binfield, was injured and Dennis played through to the Wembley final in 1968 and beyond. His exploits took him to county honours and Berks and Bucks fame. He used his large frame most effectively in protecting his goal and his whole hearted support for Chesham rightly deserves respect, as he was one of only four of the Wembley players who stayed on at Chesham after the 1967-68 season.

My first interest in the Club came in the lead up to the FA Cup run in the 1979-80 season. I remember not being able to find the ground on the night before the Cambridge game. On entering the Chess Suite with its melamine topped tables, we purchased our two tickets for Saturday's game from the Supporters' Club tea bar. Little did I know what was to follow.

I visited the Club several times in the late 1980's with sponsors. Eventually when John Pratt was manager, I had three starts in the Reserves before retiring. Once retired, I joined the board, where I was responsible for organising MFI's sponsorship and other commercial activities.

Andy Wells was the last of our family to turn out for Chesham, when he played in the early 1990's. Currently he is the last in a long line of playing members of the family, but I am sure that he will be by no means the last family member to have associations with the Club.

It was our Club Chairman, David Pembroke who approached me to write the history of the Club. It has been a gripping project and I have tried to record not only the stars of the past, but also many of the characters who have helped make the Club both on and off the field during its long and eventful existence.

One shining beacon through the years are the numbers attending games particularly some of the local derbies. Chesham won the final of the Berks and Bucks Senior Cup for the 1896-97 season, beating Marlow 2-1. The match, which was held at Maidenhead drew a crowd of 4,000.

Whilst I have tried to make the best use of my local knowledge and the records available, Chesham's long life means that much of its early story has been lost. I apologise for any errors or omissions which have arisen in consequence. If anyone has any records, mementoes or pictures which could help fill in the gaps, I should be very interested to hear from them via the Club. Who knows if a second fuller edition may one day be possible?

Peter Gibbins, February 1998

ACKNOWLEDGEMENTS

In writing the story of Chesham United FC, I have received tremendous support and assistance from many people, who have dug out information and photographs for the book and who have given me the great privilege of sharing in their memories. For the enjoyment that these have afforded me, I am most grateful.

There are three members of my family, who I must single out for special thanks. Firstly to my wife Anita, who was invaluable in assisting me during my researches and in encouraging me generally. Secondly to my sister, Zoe White, who undertook the nightmare task of typing up the text. Finally to my brother-in-law, Crispin White, who has helped me to edit and assemble the book.

I am also greatly indebted to Ray East, for his tremendous support with the pictures throughout the book and also to Bob Day for all his help.

My thanks and gratitude go to those listed below, who I hope will derive great satisfaction in seeing this history published:

Les King	Sid MacDonnell	Chesham Building Society
Bob Day	Norman Dymock	Gordon Finch
Ron Campion	Paul Campion	Christy Mulkern
Jack Dwight	Cecil Baker	Dorothy & Fred Price
Gwyn Dwight	Nigel Franklin	Jill Menghetti
Paul Vockins	Nancy Hazelhurst	John Watt
Martin Baguley	Micky Gilchrist	Steven Birkett
Tony Currie	Lisa Welling	Sir Stanley Matthews C.B.E.
Don Flitney	Maurice Payne	Margaret & Bill Wells
Steve Chambers	Martin Pritchard	Ron Richardson
Frank Dean	Jayne Denham	John & Audrey Pearce
Lyndon Berry	Frank Bunker	Wally & Heather Doman
George Piggin	David Barnes	Bob Jeffries
Christine Scott	Steve Bates	Derek & Sandra Hunt
John Armistead	Matthew Hunt	Chris Morris
Ron Hodgkins	Brian Caterer	John Reardon
Gordon Darvell	Nick Wells	Phil Devlin
Tony White	Chesham Library	Aylesbury Library

PATRONS

The profits from the sale of this book are being donated to the Riding & Driving For The Disabled Group at Bank Farm in Bellingdon. Having already raised funds for their work through a sponsored marathon golf game, I am now pleased to have a further opportunity to support the excellent work they do.

I am also indebted to the patrons of the book listed below. By subscribing for the book in advance, they ensured that its publication would be possible.

S. P. Newbury	Michael Bland	John Rance
John Gurnsey	Edwin King	R.N & C.P. Houghton
Anne Coney	Tony Adams	T. Townsend
Tony Greenham	Bob Batchelor	Ronald Nash
James Mass	Barry Holt	David Darvell
Thomas Wells	Jack Gibbins	R. W. J. Richardson
Brian Harris	Frank Bull	June Ing
Annabel Thomas	Zoe Thomas	Neil Page
Macauley Hearn	Peter Taylor	Mick Bruton & Family
Daniel White	Nicky Beasant	Sam Beasant
Sophie Beasant	Rob Gibbins	Mark Austin
Paul Ottaway	Robin Pointon	Georgina Hayes
Harriet Hayes	Joe Winterburn	Sam Carey
James Winterburn	Abbie Winterburn	Denis Bone
Johnathon Bone	Julie Bone	Geoff Williams
Gwyn Williams	Brian Caterer	Paul Skeates
Gary Bottrell	David Rothwell	Helen Rothwell
Gary Mason	Alf Stringer	Tony Van Der Bout
Nan Page	Derek Hunt	Sandra Hunt
Steve Hunt	Matt Hunt	Geoff Williams
Richard Gifford	Charlotte Gifford	Nancy Hazelhurst
Bob Day	Kasey Wells	Maurice Payne
Ray East	Bill Cleare	John Pratt
John Reardon	Bill Wells	Maragaret Wells
Robin Rackstraw	Andy Warboys	Darren Venn
David Barber	Margaret Douglas	Philip Hollett
Ray Dickerton	Ted Lewis	Gillian Rackstraw
Percy Lague	Ken Clutterbuck	Paul Vockins
Mrs Power	John Cowlinshaw	Alan Langden
John Mann	Fred King	Steve Chambers
Jim Chambers	Patrick Eggs	Eric Page

RIDING & DRIVING FOR THE DISABLED

In July 1986 Anne Coney and Gaile Ogden ran the first camp for eight physically handicapped children at Bank Farm in Bellingdon. The children had the opportunity of "owning" a pony for a week, caring for and riding it. To do this they had helpers, a minimum of two but in some severe cases three. These helpers were in the main teenagers who had given up their holidays to assist.

The camp's success lead to weekly sessions in the beginning of October 1986 for six young physically handicapped children. These children attend mainstream schools, which lack the sports facilities available at special schools and horse riding became their only sport.

Each session with the pony includes brushing, picking mud from its feet, collecting the saddle and bridle, saddling up as well as riding. These tasks can be very testing for youngsters, who have difficulty balancing normally.

The frustration, determination and achievement is fantastic to watch. The advantage of horse riding to the disabled person, whether physically or mentally handicapped, is enormous. Balance, control, determination and the affiliation between the child and the pony is now readily accepted in the medical world as a beneficial therapy, totally impossible to achieve in a hospital environment.

Success breeds fast. Immediately noticeable in school was the difference in deportment, the sudden confidence in an otherwise withdrawn child and the readiness to accept discipline, which was essential to the relationship with their pony.

The group has established itself in catering for children within a fifteen mile radius of the Bank Farm. It has just over fifty children riding, with seven disabled adults and two children driving carts.

Running the project is expensive. The needs of the riders dictate a requirement for high quality equipment. To accommodate children with spina bifida and cerebral palsy a special saddle has been developed, with a high back and handle at the front. This encourages the rider to be independent of the holding hands of the helper.

The Riding for the Disabled Group at Bank Farm, Bellingdon

Apart from the need for riding hats, the group uses mounting blocks, special reins, specially designed carts and most important of all exceptional ponies.

Ponies with a patient temperament must be selected before going through the special training necessary. Most of all the ponies must be able to stand still for long periods. Getting an adult who has suffered a stroke into a cart can take several minutes and is a delicate operation, which would end in disaster if the pony involved is restless.

The group's expenses are high. In 1996, they were running at more than £14,000 a year. In addition, after ten years, much of the safety equipment is having to be replaced, as are a number of ponies that are approaching retirement.

Riding for the Disabled Association is a registered charity, whose patron is H.R.H. The Princess Royal, G.C.V.O. Anyone who would like more information about the group can contact Anne Coney on 01494 758550 or Gaile Ogden on 01494 758027.

FOREWORD

by Sir Stanley Matthews C.B.E.

On Friday 19 May 1995, I had the great pleasure in attending Eddie Bailey's Testimonial at Chesham United FC. The game fittingly was between an Old Chesham Stars XI and an Old Tottenham Hotspur XI.

In football I have visited many non-league clubs and have always been interested in their history. Chesham has been no exception. The first football played in these parts was in 1879. This shows the local appetite for the game, from the days of Chesham Town and of course Chesham Generals, the first two senior clubs in the town. I will never forget the great cup run of 1968 playing so many matches to reach Wembley.

I've travelled the world myself as an ambassador for this great game, playing 758 league and cup matches between 1932 and 1965 excluding wartime games and have been capped 84 times for my country.

I wish everyone at CUFC the very best with the Club's history and here's to success on the field of play for many seasons to follow.

I would like to thank Peter Gibbins for inviting me to write this foreword. It's been a pleasure.

Yours in Sport,

Sign.

Sir Stanley Matthews C.B.E.

PREFACE

by David N Pembroke, Club Chairman
1994 to date

Being the Chairman of Chesham United makes me its custodian for the town and the people. Soon I will be able to pass the role on to a younger person, and I will be able to sit back and enjoy watching.

Over the years many people have given time and money to the Club , never questioning any return , except the continuation of a great little club. Many of these people will be highlighted in its history, many have been forgotten. This account of the history of Chesham United is for each and every one of them.

Today I have a dedicated and hard working board of directors, Ron Campion, Len Vockins, Tony O'Driscol, Jim Chambers, Ron Lee plus many devoted helpers.

The resurrection of the supporters club, "Friends of Chesham", is an acknowledgement of the renewal of confidence in policies that will take the Club into the Millennium.

CHAPTER 1

The Beginnings of Football in Chesham

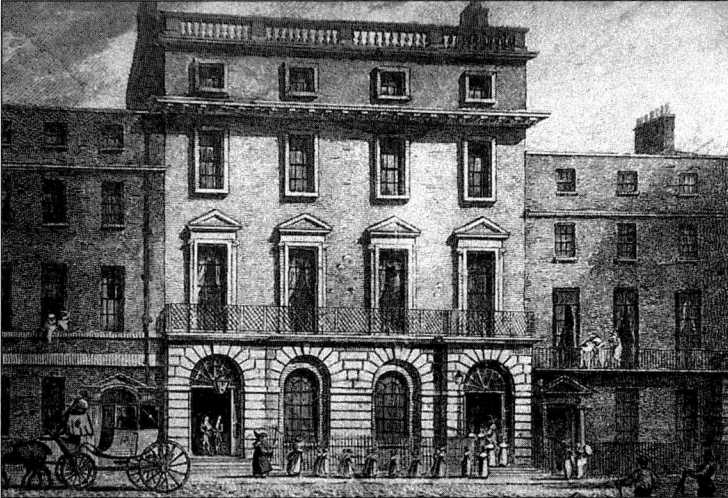

The Freemasons Tavern in Lincoln's Inn Fields, the Football Association birthplace

The Football Association was founded on 26 October 1863 and the FA Cup competition followed in 1872. It was a little time after that the first known senior team arrived in Chesham in 1879. A meeting was held on an unknown date in that year at the Mechanics' Institute in Chesham at which this important decision was taken. The meeting site is now the offices above The Chesham Building Society in Market Square. All present agreed a club should be started. Those present were all male - Messrs Clare, Hoar, Crisp, Darvell, Howard and Reverend Reade. It was decided that the Reverend Reade and Mr. Clare should act as the Club's first joint Secretaries.

The minutes of the meeting do not record the Club's name, but from subsequent minutes it appears that it was called "The Chesham and Waterside Club".

At the next committee meeting held on 2 October 1879 a set of rules were considered. The rules of the Club contained two main stipulations:

(i)   no new member be allowed to play a second time on the ground until he has paid his entrance fee and subscription and no old member until he has paid his subscription for the ensuing season. The amounts of fees were unknown.
(ii)   that no player, not a member of the Club, be allowed to play on the ground if there be 10 members of the Club present.

1880-81 season
The first recorded games were all against local opposition. The Club records having organised some eleven matches in total for the season. These games included matches with Marlow, Langley, Uxbridge, Boxmoor, Berkhamsted Grammar School and Albert United, a London club. The Club had moved its meetings to the Temperance Hotel in the Broadway, formally adopting this as its headquarters at its meeting on 8 December 1880.

The AGM in May 1881 reports that in fact 19 games were played. The Club, lead by their captain Reverend Reade, seem to have been quite successful. That season they won 11, drew 2 and lost 6. The successful games were against: Uxbridge, Albert United, Boxmoor, Boxmoor St. Georges, Wycombe, Berkhamsted, Marlow, Maidenhead, Marlow Victoria and Berkhamsted II.

Defeats were against Marlow, Wycombe, Marlow Victoria, Langley United and the Swifts (in a cup tie), with draws against Boxmoor and Berkhamsted Grammar School.

The minutes of the committee meeting on 14 October 1880 report that the Club's Secretary, Mr Clare, visited Reading Football Club the previous week to represent the Club at a committee meeting of the Berks & Bucks Association as a representative of The Chesham and Waterside Club.

The first records of any finance was the balance of accounts on 2 May 1881 when the Club had £6 19s 1d. A payment was then agreed to pay the owner of the Meadow £4 for the use of the ground. The ground was located in Missenden Road, Chesham.

The minutes record a proposal that an Athletic Association be formed in the Town on 8 December 1880 and it be called The Chesham Football & Athletic Association. It seems that the activities of the Club were incorporated into this new Association after this date. Some twenty days later on 29 December 1880 William Lowndes agreed to become the Club's first president. Lord Chesham expressed his willingness to become a Vice President.

But the Club in 1881 also had its problems and was in grave danger of folding when the shock news came that the owner of the ground Benjamin Fuller threatened to close it because of the damage caused to surrounding hedges by supporters. It was agreed to let Benjamin's son Captain Fuller persuade his father not to take the ground away. The Club also promised to renew or repair all the broken fences.

For a time it seemed that the crisis had passed, but not all was well and on 30 January 1883 a resolution was passed disbanding the Club and distributing its residual funds of £5 12s 3d.

The first minutes of Chesham Football Club, 1879

CHAPTER 2

Chesham Town FC 1879-1917

The origins of Chesham Town FC are a mystery. A Club menu for a dinner in 1922 records the Town Club as having been formed in 1879. If this were true, it is surprising that the Club's existence was not referred to at all in the minutes of the Chesham & Waterside Club and, given the restricted travel facilities of the time, difficult to imagine that some form of local derby match would not have been organised.

I suspect that later members of the Club have seen the old minute book and have assumed, without reading it in detail that it referred to Chesham Town's formation.

I have been able to trace some old photographs of a Chesham Football Club team in 1884 and 1887. In the picture is J Stone who was the long serving secretary of Chesham Town FC.

Because the minutes of the Chesham and Waterside Club become very sketchy and intermittent after mid 1881, it seems quite possible that Chesham FC was playing during the 1881-82 season and indeed this could well have hastened the demise of the earlier club.

Chesham FC 1884
Top: G Payne, F Webb, B Beckley, C Ford, A Hobbs, A Riggins, J Culverhouse, J Stone (Secretary)
Bottom: B Russell, H Rose, W Brandon, J Harrison, M Wright

In 1894 Chesham FC became founder members of the Southern League, changing their name to Chesham Town FC in 1899. Town withdrew from the Southern League in 1904.

The Club's accounts for 1902 showed gate receipts of £172 9s 8d and expenditure of £179 6s 9d. How the deficit was funded is not recorded. It was agreed that the Chesham Silver Band would play at every home fixture.

Chesham FC 1887
F Sills, F Lewis, W Sear, F Puggings, E Field, J Armstrong, W Barnell, J Stone
R Russell, A Hobbs, G Payne, J Bryant, W Brandon, J Culverhouse, H Rose

William Lowndes agreed to become the Club president, but insisted that the Club play a charity cup game with all monies being donated to the Chesham Cottage Hospital. The game raised £5 5s. Lord Rothschild, the MP for South Bucks became the Club's vice-president.

The Club's finances were improved in the next season with a profit of some £12 over the year. Unfortunately, the Club's President became ill and wrote saying he would not be able to attend matches. The Club was sharing a ground with the Chesham Cricket Club and problems began to emerge with the arrangements. Damage to the cricket table was a problem.

Another ever-present problem was the cost of insuring players, and after reviewing quotes, a policy was taken out with the General Accident & Assurance Corporation Limited. The kit

Chesham Town FC 1899-1900

worn by the Town team was produced by Gunn & Moore, better known for making cricket bats. Twelve shirts were ordered annually, the team playing in amber and black.

Local parish law only allowed goal posts flags and nets to be erected immediately after the parish church clock had struck midnight on a Friday. On many occasions the fierce local rivalry between teams lead to raids on opponents' grounds during the night.

On 1 October 1904 Town played West Ham at their new ground, Boleyn Ground, Upton Park, at the invitation of that Club's chairman, Joseph Grisdale, a local coppersmith. Local interest in the game began to grow and the Club applied to the FA for Cup Final tickets, receiving an allocation of ten for the 1905 final between Aston Villa and Newcastle. The game was played at the Crystal Palace and won by Aston Villa 2-0. Access to such games was greatly helped by the improvements to local transport, particularly the Metropolitan Line.

On 13 November 1905, Squire Lowndes, the Club's first President died. The Club sent a floral tribute in club colours and was represented at the funeral by Mr Barnes and Mr Glasgow.

In 1905 the Club undertook a Christmas football tour to Norfolk. They lost 4-1 to Ashford Town on Boxing Day and lost again the next day to Tunbridge Wells Rangers 3-0. The final game on 6 January 1906 saw Town losing 4-3 to the newly formed Norwich City FC.

On 12 March 1906 William Frith Lowndes, a nephew of William Lowndes took over as the club president and as you can see was a lover of cricket. He was captain of the county for many years. Squire Lowndes arranged many matches in the closed season with many notables appearing such as Dr W G Grace, his last visit being 1907, when a crowd of 500 came to see him at Chesham.

William Frith Lowndes in cricket gear

Crowds caused trouble even in 1906. A club report from 16 March showed a disturbance at a game, when the referee was attacked and two local men, Albert Brandon and Sherringham were banned from the ground. On March 12th Shifs and Stephenson were on FA charges of misconduct and Chesham's ground was closed. The FA report of 19 March 1906 read as follows:

"South Eastern League and Chesham

At a meeting of the management committee of the South-Eastern League held at the George Hotel, Strand, yesterday evening, the principal business discussed was the playing of the home matches of the Chesham Town FC through the closing of their ground.

The suspension was passed owing to the behaviour of a section of the crowd towards the referee, Mr. A.J.Kips, who was struck by one of the spectators.

The league sanctioned the playing of the remainder of Chesham's home engagements on their opponents' grounds.

This will mean a visit to Sittingbourne, Tunbridge Wells, and West Hampstead, the league having decided that the offence of the penalised club was not bad enough to further punish them, and they will finish the season without further discomfort than the loss of the gates mentioned."

The 1906 Annual Meeting presided over by Mr N M Plummer was held at the Victoria Rooms in the Crown Hotel. It was reported by the secretary that the Club had played fairly well despite problems with crowd trouble. The Club reached the final of the newly formed Bucks Charity Cup which they lost to Aylesbury United. The ground was suspended in March, leading to lost gates of £10 9s 8d.

BALANCE SHEET, SEASON 1905-1906.

RECEIPTS.	£ s. d.		EXPENDITURE.	£ s. d.	
To Balance from Season 1904–05	43 7 0		By amount transferred to Reserve	35 0 0	
„ Subscriptions from Clubs and Competitions	32 10 0		„ Outstanding accounts for 1904-05	1 12 3	
„ Entry Fees to Cup Competitions	24 2 6		„ COUNTY MATCHES—		
„ Referees' Subscriptions and Entry Fees	32 15 0		Seniors v. Herts, at Aylesbury ... 13 15 1		
„ Subscription for appointing Referees	0 10 6		„ v. Middlesex, at Wycombe 9 11 0		
„ Vice-Presidents' Subscriptions	17 5 6		„ v. Surrey, at Guildford... 5 17 9		
„ Protest Fees and Fines	12 5 6		„ v. Suffolk, at Ipswich 10 19 5		
„ GATE RECEIPTS—COUNTY MATCHES—			Juniors v. London Juniors, at		
Seniors v. Herts, At Aylesbury... 7 19 7			Windsor 5 5 10		
„ v. Middlesex, at Wycombe 5 16 2			„ v. Middlesex Juniors, at Slough 4 12 10		
„ v. Suffolk, at Ipswich (share) 7 0 0				50 1 11	
Juniors v. London Juniors, at Windsor 1 9 4			„ SENIOR CUP—		
Juniors v. Middlesex Juniors, at Slough 2 2 0			Semi-final—Reading Amateurs v. Chesham Town, at Maidenhead 10 9 1		
	24 7 1		Semi-final — Maidenhead Norfolkians v. Wycombe Wanderers, at Marlow 16 5 0		
„ SENIOR CUP—			Ditto—Re-play 18 8 2		
Semi-final—Reading Amateurs v. Chesham Town, at Maidenhead 11 2 8			Final—Reading Amateurs v. Maidenhead Norfolkians, at Slough... 36 7 0		
Semi-final—Maidenhead Norfolkians v. Wycombe Wanderers, at Marlow 24 17 0				81 9 3	
Ditto—Re-play 59 6 11			„ JUNIOR CUP—		
Final — Reading Amateurs v. Maidenhead Norfolkians, at Slough 120 1 0			Semi-final—Slough Reserves v. Chesham Town Reserves, at Aylesbury 6 19 6		
	215 7 7		Semi-final—Reading Grovelands v. Stokenchurch, at Wallingford... 5 7 4		
„ JUNIOR CUP—			Final — Reading Grovelands v. Slough Reserves, at Maidenhead 8 5 3		
Semi-final—Slough Reserves v. Chesham Town Reserves, at Aylesbury 2 3 4			Ditto—Re-play) 7 19 5		
Semi-final—Reading Grovelands v. Stokenchurch, at Wallingford 5 4 10				28 11 6	
Final—Reading Grovelands v. Slough Reserves, at Maidenhead 6 15 9			„ MINOR CUP—		
Ditto—Re-play 10 11 7			Final—Newport Pagnell Reserves v. Reading Defiance, at Abingdon 9 5 3		
	24 15 6		„ Subscriptions to F.A. and Southern Counties Championship, 1906-07 1 1 0		
„ MINOR CUP—			„ Protest Fees returned 4 12 6		
Final — Newport Pagnell Reserves v. Reading Defiance, at Abingdon 10 17 10			„ Medals (Vaughton's account) 25 17 0		
„ Sale of Referees' Badges 0 4 6			„ Badges for County Players 4 0 0		
„ Sale of Handbooks 0 17 0			„ Secretary 40 0 0		
„ Interest on Reserve Fund 4 4 1			„ Printing 23 16 0		
„ Sundry Receipts 0 5 0			„ Fares to Meetings 36 18 4		
			„ Hire of Rooms for Meetings 5 11 3		
			„ Stamps, telegrams, stationery, etc. 14 7 5		
			„ Referees' Charts 1 13 4		
			„ Expenses of Referees' Committees 2 6 10		
			„ Auditors' Fees 1 1 0		
			„ Sundry small accounts 1 10 7		
			„ Amounts due to Clubs under Senior Cup rule 29—		
			Maidenhead Norfolkians 16 15 0		
			Reading Amateurs 10 10 0		
			Wycombe Wanderers 6 5 0		
				33 10 0	
			„ Balance at Bank 41 9 2		
	£443 14 7			£443 14 7	

There is also a sum of £185 invested in the Post Office Savings Bank.

R. A. LUNNON, Hon. Treasurer.

Balance Sheet, Season 1905-1906

Chesham Town FC 1907-1908

The 1907 annual meeting was also held at the Victoria Rooms. It was described as "a year of incident from start to finish". The opening day fixture against Grays was a no show and Grays disbanded shortly after. On the last Saturday of the season Tunbridge Wells got lost in London. On 9 February the referee at the Berks & Bucks semi final, Mr McDonald, reported the Chesham crowd (nicknamed The Tea Room Boys) for bad behaviour. Chesham lost 4-2 after a replay. An approach was made to Chesham for Tommy Stillman, and he received a trial on Easter Monday at Fulham FC. This season Chesham played QPR and Crystal Palace in friendlies.

On Easter Monday 20 April 1907 Chesham won the Berks & Bucks at Wycombe beating Windsor and Eton 2-0. A fixture with Woolwich Arsenal was proposed, but the Club received a telegram to say no fixture was available.

On 9 November Lord Chesham the Club President died in a riding accident in Northamptonshire. He had been born as Charles Compton Cavendish on 13 September 1850.

In 1908 an extraordinary meeting was held to resolve problems with the ground, involving both the football and cricket clubs. It was proposed that a tenancy be set up for a lease of up to 14 years until 1921 to "embrace all sports". On 28 March the final of the Berks & Bucks Junior Cup was played against Reading, at Loakes Park, High Wycombe. Reading won 3-1, and a train service was put on with trains leaving at 12.07 from Chesham. It was quite a notable season, with Chesham winning the South-Eastern League.

The League decided to divide into two sections A and B. Chesham was placed in the B section with Hastings, St Leonards, Kettering, Romford, Peterborough City and South Farnborough. The clubs were able to appoint their own linesmen and the winners of each section would play a final against each other. It was agreed that travel expenses would be paid to travelling teams.

12 April 1909 saw the Berks & Bucks Cup Final at Marlow which Chesham lost to Wycombe 3-0.

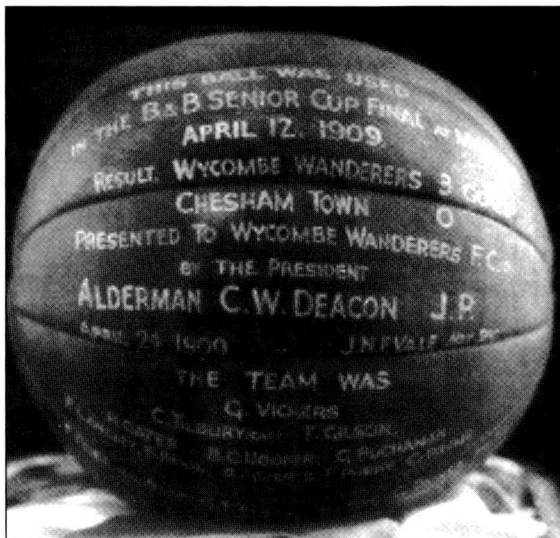

Commemorative football from the 1909 Berks and Bucks Cup Final,
now kept in the boardroom at Wycombe Wanderers.

The years from 1910 until the amalgamation of the two local clubs were not eventful for Chesham Town FC and the onset of war caused a major reduction in activities.

The building of the War Memorial in Chesham

CHAPTER 3

Chesham Generals FC 1887-1917

Chesham General Baptist Church

In 1887 a club was formed by the Young Men's' Mutual Improvement Class of the General Baptist Chapel. The team took their name, "The Generals", from the Chapel which was located in the Broadway. As the early picture above shows the Chapel's appearance then differs greatly today's. The Club was formed to play football in the winter and cricket in the summer. Its captain was Mr. Harry Ellement and its first honorary secretary George Webb.

Chesham General Baptist Church

For a short period the Club's ground was in the Top Park, followed by two seasons at Portobello Farm. Then after playing for several years in Bellingdon Road, the Club required better accommodation and moved to the New Town Ground, which was also known as the Co-op Ground, Brockhurst Road.

The last two decades of the nineteenth century saw a boom in amateur football with many local clubs being formed. During the period from 1887 to 1890 only local matches were played.

1888-89 season

16 matches were played against teams including Boxmoor, Maidenhead, Wycombe and Uxbridge. The Generals won 11, lost 3 and drew 2.

1889-90 season

The Club produced its first fixture card using its original name of Chesham General Baptist FC and played 31 matches.

The season saw their first visit to High Wycombe in a friendly on 16 November. The previous week Wycombe had beaten Wycombe Trinity 13-0 at home. Their home ground was the site now occupied by the cricket ground on the London Road in High Wycombe. They had just secured a headquarters at the Nags Head public house opposite the ground, which was used as changing rooms. Wycombe then had some 30 players on its books. This was only Wycombe's 28th game and they beat the Generals 3-0, with two goals scored by A Lane and one by Morris. Sid Morris had only recently defected from another Wycombe team and this created much bad feeling.

A return match was agreed and Wycombe visited Chesham on 28 December 1889. After a difficult two hour journey by horse transport they lost 1-0 to the Generals.

1890-91 season
The Club's membership had been limited to attendees of the General Baptist Chapel, but in this season it was decided to throw membership open, resulting in a large influx of new members. The Club joined the Berks & Bucks Football Association and entered the Berks & Bucks Junior Cup. The Club won prizes at both junior level and at an early season 6 a side competition at Berkhamsted.

1891-92 season
36 matches were played.

1892-93 season
Two experienced players A. Hobbs and F. G. Racklyeft threw in their lot with the Generals. The Club now moved from the Co-op Ground to the New Town Ground. The opening match was against the Old Sherbrookians. This season they entered the English Cup competition playing Maidenhead in the first round. The Club also entered the Luton Charity Cup and reached the semi final of the Berks & Bucks Junior Cup, which it lost to the Grenadier Guards.

Transport to an early match

1893-94 season
The Generals ventured into the Amateur Cup competition for the first time. The team were drawn against Reading, then a professional side which fielded an amateur second team. The Generals lost 1-0, but were not disgraced by the outcome. As a good gate was guaranteed for the match the team waived the choice of ground. The season was also memorable for the election of Mr. Hawes to the Berks & Bucks County FA.

Teams of professional sides, such as Millwall and Spurs, now visited Chesham quite regularly for friendly games. Players were paid expenses of one shilling (5 new pence) per match tea money, but more usually bought a pint of beer and bread for four old pence, showing an eight pence profit. Transport to away games outside Chesham was horse drawn. The hilly local area meant that players would frequently need to disembark from the horse drawn brakes to reduce the load on the horse going up steep hills or to enable their descent to be controlled coming down.

Chesham Generals FC 1st XI 1897-98

Chesham Generals Reserves 1897-98
The team to bring the first trophy to Chesham, as winners of the 1897 Aylesbury & District League Cup

1897-98 season

The numbers of players available enabled a reserves side to be formed, which played its first game on 8 November 1897 against Wycombe, losing 3-1.

On 20 September 1897 a crowd of 250 watched the first team entertain Wycombe for their first game of the season, which the Generals lost 4-1, although they beat Wycombe at home 4-0 at their next meeting on 7 February 1898.

The reserves met Wycombe again in January 1898 in the third round of the Berks & Bucks Junior Cup, losing 3-2. This was in a severely cold winter with the Thames freezing at Henley.

1900-1902

Arthur Rance, an early Generals goalkeeper, wrote in 1965 of some of his memories. The Generals won the Berks & Bucks Cup for the first time in the 1900-1901 season and he recalls the team being paraded round the town in a horse brake with a band in front and with Lord Chesham standing outside the Town Hall as they passed.

Chesham Generals FC 1900-1901

Chesham Generals 1902-1903

The next season they nearly reached the Amateur Cup final of 1902. The match was playedat Leeds that year, Wembley only have been used since 1949. The Generals lost in the semi final 4-2 to the Old Malvernians, who went on to win the final against Bishop Auckland 5-1.

Chesham Generals 1902-1903

Chesham Generals Reserves 1903-1904

1902-1917

The period from 1902 until 1917's amalgamation was not too successful for the Generals, who featured quite regularly at the bottom of the league. Even so the local press reported the Club's activities in some detail as was noted in the Secretary's report of 3 September 1909.

After some searching I found an original Generals shirt dating back to 1910. The Generals wore a shirt made by Rileys of Altrincham Manchester, a company better known for making snooker and cricket equipment.

Chesham Generals Reserves 1904-1905

Chesham Generals 1908-1909

Chesham Generals 1909-1910

Chesham Generals 1910-1911

Chesham Generals 1913-1914
Spartan League Champions

Chesham Generals in action at Brockhurst Road

The Chesham Generals Goalkeeper clears the danger

Brockhurst Road Ground showing the Waterworks in the background

With modern communications transport to matches was much improved

The first Chesham United team 1917
Bill Holloman, Fred Wilson, Laurie Webb, Charlie Moulder, Cyril Webb, Frank Brandon,
Sid Darvell, Ted Hunnibell, George Darvell, Horace Reading, Herbert Bruton,
Jack Ringsell, Sid Gomm, Sonny Morton, Joe King, Frank Hayes

CHAPTER 4

The Birth of Chesham United FC 1917-1920

An early proposal to amalgamate the two Clubs was put forward in 1902. A meeting to discuss the matter was held at Chess Vale School on 25 August 1902. It was suggested that if the two Clubs joined forces they could provide competition to the better local teams, Wycombe, Watford and Reading.

The idea was that each Club would have equal representation on the Board of Management with the Club Chairman having no ties to either. After prolonged discussions into the early hours of the morning at an open meeting held on 3 September at the Mechanics Institute, agreement could not be reached and the Clubs remained independent.

Players lost in the First World War
Both teams lost players during the Great War of 1914 - 1918. Those recorded were:
J Barnes, F P Brackley, F Gomm, W Gomm, F J Hyatt, F Hayes, S Holt, P E Hunnibell, J Jones, P J Keen, A M Mayo, C Mayo and A Rance.

The General's non-playing secretary A M Mayo was killed in France by a shell. He was closely connected with the railway at Chesham, having set up the cartage company, Crook & Mayo.

The decision to amalgamate the two teams was the logical solution to the shortage of players caused by so many of the fitter men being away at war and the sad losses of those terrible years. At one stage it had even been necessary to post an advert for players.

The ball started rolling with the formation of an Advisory Committee. One meeting records the assets each Club could contribute.

Chesham Town offered:

	£	s
Pavilion	25	0
Dressing room	10	0
Pay box	1	0
Pitch roller	10	0
Total	46	0

The Generals offered:

	£	s
Pavilion and stand	23	10
Pay box	4	10
2 brooms, 2 tables, 1 pail, 2 wheelbarrows, 7 bowls & 14 footballs	3	10
Total	31	10

Eventually it was decided not to purchase the pavilion and stand from The Generals but to purchase the pay box and transfer it from the Bellingdon Road Ground, another Generals' ground, to the Cricket and Sports Ground at The Meadow.

The football ground used by The Generals in Berkhamsted Road was now disused and was only used for fetes and open air concerts.

The Generals' Disused Ground

News of the two clubs joining sparked a real interest in finishing the games the war had held up. The Generals' Meadow ground in Bellingdon Road had been loaned to local football clubs by the Co-op Society who owned the ground. This made a good site for the Chesham Cup Final between Caleys and Rovers.

Chesham Generals Ground (disused) which formed
the first Council Estate in Chesham in the 1930s

The choice of ground caused some problems. Several sites were discussed by the committee and with local land owners. The old Generals' ground, the old ground in Berkhamsted Road, Home Farm owned by Mr Rose and a site called Red Meadow were all possibilities.

Mr Rose was asking for £5 and repairs to hedges and fences for a "good season". But Frogmore Meadow, Pednor was initially decided upon although it was more expensive at £10 a season, but seemed more accessible. Trial matches were organised to look at young local talent. Selected players paid 1s 3d per head as a joining fee.

The changing rooms were at The Queens Head in Church Street, in Old Chesham. A separate area for referees to change in had to be provided and towels purchased. Four footballs were purchased at a cost of 27s 6d. The goal posts and nets had to be renewed due to the wear and tear of the war years.

The true birth date of Chesham United FC is uncertain. Its first match appears to have been on Saturday 3rd November 1917 when a friendly match was arranged between The Royal Garrison and Artillery Signal Depot XI, stationed at Halton Camp, and Chesham United. United lost 5-2. The match was played on the "Pig Trough" as Chesham's second meadow is named. It had been quickly organised by the new secretary, Mr J G Stone and Frank Hayes.

The Chesham team was as follows: Laurie Webb (in his old position in goal), King, Wingrove, Joe King, Charlie Moulder (once more in his old place), Frank Brandon, Horace Reading (still with plenty of vim), Sid Gomm, Wright, Frank Hayes, George Hawes with G Darvell as whistle blower.

SPEC, the editor of The Examiner, saw the game like this: "The visitors had an officer in goal who knew something of the rugby code, an ex-Celtic at the back, at centre half, a Birmingham man and a good one. The visitors won 5-2 after leading by 3-0 and the spectators and the Chesham Team ungrudgingly acknowledged that they were full value for money. Hefty with plenty of weight to cope with the heavy ground, they trapped a ball cleverly, swung it about with ease and were speedy in their tracks for goal. Webb had to handle some real beauties and had small chance with shots that scored, four of the five goals being directly attributable to Kirkham. Chesham provided the soldiers with a nice game. Both the Chesham goals by Hawes and Hayes were good. The conditions were hazy and the ground heavy, but the match provided an afternoon's most welcome sport."

Minutes of the first Committee Meeting of Chesham United

The Club's first committee meeting was recorded on Tuesday 20 November 1917. The club was formally recognised by the FA and the Berks & Bucks FA with effect from 1 December 1917 and this must be regarded as its official birth date. The first committee were the following:

H A V Byrne (chairman), J G Stone (secretary), F J Wilson (treasurer), W Hawes, H Lacey, E Hunnibel, W White, C Webb, W J Humphrey, R Beckley, W Holliman, H Smith, J Wood, F Keen and G Darvell.

To ensure the continuity of policy, the committee was appointed to hold office until the 1st day of August in the third year following the recommencement of official football.

Colours adopted by the new Club were claret and blue, as Aston Villa not West Ham. Gunn & Moore had the contract to supply the playing kit, but only new shirts were purchased annually at a cost of £4 2s 6d. The ground first chosen was Chesham Sports Ground, generally known as Chesham Cricket Ground.

As peace arrived activity increased. Travel to away games was now usually by motor car, but many longer trips still meant very early starts.

With interest growing all the time, a supporters' association was set up to help with the administration on match days. The first private enterprise was set up by Mr Maerchant, a local man who sold chocolate and eventually cups of tea. This brought in much needed revenue of £3 3s per annum.

Problems with supporters continued. A letter was received from Mrs Darvell expressing much concern that her crop of apples was being stolen by supporters climbing over her fence during matches.

Mr W F Lowndes was approached to support help in building a stand and dressing rooms. These were planned to be 20 feet by 10 feet in size, with full plumbing and with gas laid on. Tradesmen were contacted to provide quotations and delivery times. One highlight was that Ladies would be allowed in the enclosure free of charge, except for cup games.

The first public meeting of Chesham United was extensively reported in the Examiner in August 1919.

1919-20 season

As the Examiner reported in May 1920 the first season of Chesham United FC after the amalgamation "began gloriously and ended poorly". The team won the Bucks Charity Cup and did well in other cup competitions, but its league record speaks for itself. When Chesham were winning cups, they could not be playing league matches.

On 10 October 1919 the first Amateur Cup tie pulled in a splendid crowd of well over 1,000. Played against Uxbridge Town on a day more fit for cricket at the Cricket Meadow, Chesham cruised to a club record high score of 8-0. The previous three results had been wins of 5-0 against Yiewsley, 6-0 against Newportians and 8-0 against Tufnell Spartans, so Laurie Webb in the Chesham goal was responsible for a string of safe games.

Chesham then proceeded in the competition to beat Wealdstone 4-2, Yiewsley 1-5, Hampstead 1-2, succeeding where Wycombe failed, Aylesbury 2-0 and Bromley 0-5.

Overall it was a season of strange results. United's first visit to Loakes Park, High Wycombe resulted in a 6-0 thrashing on 26 December, but at Chesham the following day United won 3-2 after conceding a penalty to A Smith.

CHAPTER 5

The Glorious Twenties 1920-1930

1920-21 season

The Club's rebuilding of its playing staff was in full swing, although league results remained disappointing. George Barnes was unanimously elected as Club Captain for the coming season, although he was still doubling up for Watford's Reserves between Chesham games. One new addition to the team was Eric Woolford.

1921-22 season

Chesham's double was headline news in the Spartan League, Chesham winning the league's first division on goal difference and the reserves winning the second division. The League's Secretary R M Price reported:

"All praise is due to Chesham United for their magnificent finish. Few teams could have come through such a trying time with such wonderful success, a success which must be attributed to their splendid condition and finish. They are worthy champions of our league. It must certainly be recorded also that our champions defeated Wycombe Wanderers at the second attempt in the final of the Berks & Bucks Senior Cup final at Slough in front of a record 10,000 people and gate money of nearly £590. Yet a third honour secured by this fine Chesham team was the Bucks Charity Cup, a trophy competed for by seven teams in the county of Bucks."

He also reported that the trophy (the Dunbar Cup) presented by Lord Burnham the Spartan League's President had been won by the Reserves. Chesham hosted the rest of the league in the annual challenge match, being defeated 1-0, but the outstanding display recorded was the one by the keeper, Taylor who had a truly brilliant game in goal.

Chesham United 1921-1922

The Spartan League minutes record several interesting snippets. In the Berks & Bucks Cup final Chesham defeated Wycombe Wanderers 2-0 after a 1-1 draw on Easter Monday watched by 10,000, a record gate. In the Bucks Charity Cup Wolverton were beaten 1-0. The last four matches were played in six days.

Annual subscriptions to the League were £2 2s for Division I and £1 15s for Division II. League rules required all matches to be played on enclosed grounds. If a match was aborted due to fog, rain etc., the visiting team would receive half of their actual third class railway fares when the match was played. Referees in Division I were allowed 10s 6d travelling expenses, those in Division II 5s. Only half fees were paid for a postponed game. A resolution was passed on 31 May 1921 that "no reinstated professional shall be permitted to play in Spartan League games".

Cups won by Chesham United 1921-1922 season

The victorious Chesham teams were as follows :

The First Eleven: A C Taylor (goalkeeper-a wizard in his day); W Brandon and F Pearson ("Dilling" and Fred, a tough pair); Harold Dean, Arthur Gomm, and Tom Stillman (halves-a strong line); Ron Garton, Polly Perkins, Dick Lacey, Cpl A W Oakes, and George H Barnes (a scoring line of forwards, with youth on their side).

The Second Eleven group were: Cyril Webb (goalkeeper-the old Generals' keeper); H Redding and S Ringsell; G Hammond, A Wright, and Chris Rance; Maurice Barnes, Eric Woolford, J Rogers, A Rogers, F Filby and Sid Rance.

The Chesham team of the 1921-22 season was truly one of the best with six cups on the sideboard and two senior county cups.

The Club Secretary in his memoirs wrote "it was the greatest season in his experience of some 43 years of connection with football in Chesham, with such youngsters as 23 year old George Barnes, 22 year old "Polly" Perkins, 20 year old Dick Lacey and 18 year old Ron Garton. The team also included some veterans such as W (Dilling) Brandon who was 37 and Tom Stillman who had stepped up some 14 years previously to take his Berks & Bucks Cup medal.

This season saw a start of programmes at matches.

There were two deaths in 1921-22, the Chairman Mr H A V Byrne, who was 60 years and died of kidney failure and Mr J Wood, a committee member. A special dinner was arranged on Tuesday 30 May 1922 to celebrate the season's great triumphs, chaired by the new Chairman H

Chesham United Committee 1921-1922

J Turner. The Spartan League was represented by J R Schumacher, honorary secretary and treasurer. The Club's game with Oxford City created such interest that it was filmed and later shown at the Palace Cinema in the Town on the same day at 5.15pm, 7pm and 9pm. The first day trip excursion was planned by the supporters' association to the first Cup match at Ilford and was priced at 4s 5d.

This season also saw George Barnes, the Club Captain selected for the FA team to play against Cambridge University.

1922-23 season
The Spartan League was won for the second successive year, as was the Bucks Charity Cup. The Club were winners of the Apsley Senior Charity Cup. In a special match on Saturday 14 April 1923 Chesham United played the rest of the league winning 5-2. The Club received many letters praising the Captain, George Barnes and his team for putting Chesham firmly on the football map, not least for inflicting a 14-0 defeat on Maidenhead, still a record for that club.

The Club's financial position looked good at the end of this successful season so the Club was able to invest in a new pavilion which cost £988.

1923-24 season
After several seasons of success the tables were turned. This was a bad year financially with a drop in gate money because of the lack of success. The team were hit by several injuries so that more players had to used than usual. On the plus side a lot of prospective young talent was emerging locally and it was decided to run a third team for the following season after the Club's AGM. Four Club stalwarts left, Arthur Mills, A C Taylor, Dick Lacey, and Corporal Oakes and the Club's Secretary had to stand down after an association with local football since 1880. The Bucks Charity Cup and Bucks Hospital Cup were both won.

To join the club as a member would cost you 18d as well as your gate fee per game. The Club's ground share with the Cricket Club was not working because the two seasons overlapped. Discussions began to try to resolve this problem and a new ground began to be considered.

1924-25 season

A successful season with 3 trophies won. The first was the Bucks Senior Charity Cup played at Aylesbury, Chesham beating Wolverton 1-0 after a replay. 2,000 supporters looked on. The league title was won several games before the season's end. The final league match was away at Sutton Court. The team won the final game of the season against Aylesbury United in the Aylesbury Hospital Cup final. The Juniors won the Berks & Bucks Junior Cup final.

Chesham United 1924-1925

The season was marred by the death of Maurice Barnes, George Barnes' brother and a regular for the reserves, on 8 November 1924. He was knocked out in a collision with C Care of Maidenhead and died without ever regaining consciousness after an operation at Chesham Cottage Hospital later the same day.

1925-26 season

Some debate raged over the inclusion of Chesham United in the league for the season. A jealous element of the Essex clubs tried to oppose the invitation to Chesham to reapply, which was then required annually. "Chesham folk were puzzled by the way they were left out in the cold". A meeting to resolve this situation was called by the Spartan League on 5 June 1925 and the problem resolved. A and B geographical sections of 15 clubs were set up with the inclusion of Colchester Town, a giant amongst Essex amateur football in Chesham's section. Minimising travel expenses was a key point to this reorganisation, the trip to Colchester away being a day out on the Great Eastern Railway.

Chesham's first home game of the season on 19 September against Hertford Town showed off L F Dewick (in goal), previously a well known face to Watford supporters. Chesham won 4-2.

1926-27 season

An unexceptional season. As the league table shows, good defending could not compensate for lack of fire power in attack.

1927-28 season

A disappointing season though the Wycombe Hospital Cup was bought to Chesham for the first time. The Bucks Charity Cup was also won, as was the Berks & Bucks Junior Cup. The ground was the big story of the year. The Club Chairman W F Lowndes felt that all clubs should have their own ground and that the Club would not prosper locally without it. Whatever he could do to help would be done.

Chesham United 1927-1928

Chesham United "A" Team 1927-1928

The goal scorers tally makes interesting reading with a total of 149 goals scored in the season in league and cup games. In previous years this would have put Chesham in championship position again scoring over 100 goals, but the quality of the defence still show through with only 44 goals conceded.

George Barnes' reappearance on the wing was invaluable. The gates were still "fair" with finances well into the black "better than most allied counties clubs".

Chesham United 1928-1929

1928-29 season

This was an epic year in the FA Cup. In the third qualifying round Chesham played Finchley in three entertaining games, ending up with a trip to Vicarage Road. Eventually after 330 minutes of football Chesham won 5-1. The game was ranked as United's "best so far".

Watford also got the message loud and clear when in February a home game with Watford Old Boys netted an 11-0 victory.

FA Cup dreams ended in November with a 2-1 away defeat by Southall, but the success carried on in the Berks & Bucks Senior Cup with a 3-0 home win against Windsor and Eton. A tricky away fixture against Wycombe Wanderers at Aylesbury was won 2-1. On Easter Monday, the final was played against Aylesbury United at Loakes Park, Chesham victorious by 7-1. Aylesbury entered a protest against the inclusion of "Polly" Perkins in the Chesham team and the Berks & Bucks FA ruled that the match be replayed, with Chesham winning this time by 3-1. The Wycombe Hospital Cup was also won.

1929-30 season

Chesham shocked Isthmian League champions Nunhead in the FA Amateur Cup beating them away 3-1 in the second round. The division was renamed the Spartan League Premier Division and a new Division 1 introduced.

The question of the ground still loomed with the games in the first and last months of the season still played away from the home ground to leave it free for cricket.

At the club celebration dinner held at the Town Hall on Friday 20 June 1930 the Club's Chairman W F Lowndes Esq made an important statement relating to Chesham sports ground. He spoke of the great anxiety that had been caused by the shared ground and the need not only to succour football but cricket as well. He went on to speak about his late uncle Squire Lowndes and his love for local sport and his feeling that a sports ground should be available for all time. By securing two sports meadows he would be remembered for all time. He suggested a trust must be formed to protect these meadows for the Town. He paid tributes to Mr Howard and Mr Francis of Howard Son & Gooch, the Estate Agents, for their hearty support stressing that without these two it would not have been possible to secure the freehold of the meadows, which were the only level piece of ground adjacent to the Town and convenient for sport that was available.

Chesham United 1929-1930

Lord Chesham, one of the Club's presidents explained the ground situation to the Club AGM thus: "Mr Lowndes has been very generous paying the necessary deposit, a sports ground has been obtained for the town in perpetuity. The cost of the ground apart from improvements was £2,000 and this sum it was proposed to raise by donations. This would be raised by forming a company." The Football Club committee donated their £172 on deposit.

This season the Club won the Bucks Charity Senior and Junior Cups, the Chesham Challenge Cup and the High Wycombe Hospital Cup.

George Barnes became the first playing member of a league club to be elected a Vice-President of the Spartan League during his playing career.

CHAPTER 6

Third Class 1930-1947

1930-31 season

The Club's entry for the FA Cup was not forthcoming because no ground was available in September when the preliminary game should have been played. £150 was raised to improve the Club heating system, which resulted in a totally new system being installed in the dressing rooms and to improve the accommodation for spectators. Reverend Reade, one of the original founders of football in Chesham, died.

Hodgson Limited of London and Nottingham at work laying the new pitch

On 24 April 1931 "Four Thousand Shillings Wanted!" was the headline. The Club was in the unfortunate position that it could not use the new ground until the playing area was fenced in and money was needed to carry out these works.

A Home For Sport Has Been Purchased

The new ground was opened with a Spartan League fixture against Slough on 31 October 1931. It was designed and built to the highest specifications available to accommodate thousands rather than hundreds of supporters. In comfortable surroundings away from traffic set among the trees, it had a magnificent playing space 75 yards by 115 yards in extent, which is still the largest playing surface in non-league football.

The local press reported: "The ground lies in a basin, the rim affords terracing for a large company of spectators. From the road to the stand there is a good firm hard core way and as far as the entrance to the football meadow is concerned motor vehicles will find it excellent to approach and they can park both left and right. The right hand side is terraced and surmounted by a stand, giving three tiers of terracing and a good approach to the enclosure and stand. The top part of the ground has been banked and has a stand, the left hand side is a natural terrace, the bottom (Cow Meadow End) again forms natural terracing. Spectators can ring the ground and all be in comfort and all see. The stand gives a commanding view of all the ground, corner flags and all. The stand has been improved since its removal from the cricket field with more seats provided.

At the rear have been built dressing rooms and a committee room between which the dressing rooms have been built, both very spacious. They are fitted with big deep concrete baths served with hot and cold water with a shower attached. A boiler house had been fitted with an "Ideal" boiler above which were cylindrical tanks, one which contains 300 gallons of hot water, and the other a similar quantity of cold water. The room for the referee and linesmen is fitted with a bath and hot and cold water. As before installation of the rebuilt stand the players approach the dressing rooms from the centre of the stand. The players enter the field of play descending a flight of steps to the playing area. The concrete bed of the stand, extending beyond the stand itself makes one roomy line of terracing. The enclosure was railed in oak paled fence, inside is a tea hut, which provides refreshment at the interval. The ground is constructed with an 18" drop each way from the centre to assist drainage. A great amount of care had been taken with regard

Programme for Opening Day 31 October 1931

to the drainage. There are underground drains running three sides of the meadow and running clean through the middle of the ground. There were many soakaways, five beneath the middle length of the ground and more at the sides. Several weather conditions like snow and heavy rain had been taken into consideration. The construction company was Messrs. Hodgson Limited of Nottingham and the design was prepared by London architects F E Howard and Sons."

Pictures of work on the ground show how much manual work was involved, with most carried out using shovels, picks, spades and wheelbarrows and no digging out by machine. Hodgsons were well know sports ground builders, and they were assisted by Mr George Payne and Mr Frank Payne, the Club's groundsmen. George Payne was the groundsman of both the cricket and football clubs in 1930. The job was a part-time appointment and he was paid for his work. The goal nets were put up every game due to their composition. Nets were cotton that didn't

Opening of the New Football Ground

OCTOBER 31st, 1931.

ORDER OF OPENING CEREMONY at 2.45 p.m.

Mr. J. G. STONE (Hon. Sec.) will introduce CAPTAIN THE RIGHT HON. LORD CHESHAM, M.C., and ask him to declare the Ground open.
Mr. G. H. BARNES (Chairman of Committee) will propose a vote of thanks to his Lordship.
Mr. THOS. LYLE (Chairman Berks & Bucks F.C. and Spartan League) will second vote of thanks.
CAPTAIN THE RIGHT HON. LORD CHESHAM, M.C. will lead the players on to the field, cut the ribbons for their entry to playing pitch and proceed to the centre to kick off.

TO-DAY IS OUR GREAT DAY. Thanks to the persistence and interest of Mr. LOWNDES, C.hesham United Football Club now have a Ground worthy of the Club and its history, and one which can be entirely devoted to football and allied sports. We think all our supporters will agree that we **have a** Ground which the Club, the supporters, the town, and the whole district may be proud. Messrs. HODGSON, the contractors; and Messrs. F. E. HOWARD & SONS, the architects and surveyors, are to be cordially congratulated on the lay-out of the Ground. The Club, on their part, have not spared trouble or expense in making the fittings of the Ground complete and up-to-date, and when the work is entirely finished it will satisfy everybody. To equip the Ground has, of course, meant a great expense. To meet this expense a public appeal has been made for funds, and so far has met with a generous response, but more money is still needed, and the subscription list is still open. The Committee wish to extend cordial thanks to all those supporters who gave freely in materials and labour to help in making the approach road to the Ground, and the confidently appeal for the continued support of the public in their effort to supply good sport for the district.

We cordially welcome LORD CHESHAM our enthusiastic and sporting helper. He has kindly consented to open the Ground, and no more fitting choice of an opener could be made. We deeply regret that our other president, Mr. Lowndes, cannot be present, owing to indisposition, but we know that he is with us in spirit and sympathy, and we all wish him a speedy restoration to health.

Souvenir Rosettes of the Club Colours will be on sale to-day. Buy one from the ladies, and so celebrate this auspicious occasion.

Yours faithfully,
THE COMMITTEE.

Lord Chesham leads the players on to the New Ground

weather very well. All the equipment was stored under the stand. The other main job on match days was lighting of the copper for hot water for the baths. When Lord Chesham severed the claret and the blue ribbon and let the two teams out on to the pitch for the first time, it heralded a new era in Chesham sports. It was the end of a long saga in providing a much needed facility. The one regret on the day was the absence of the Club's benefactor, Mr W F Lowndes. A telegram from him read at the opening went as follows: "Very sorry not to be at the opening today. I hope the new ground will prove all that is desired, and I send congratulations to the Club on their successes so far this season and wish them continued success". Good wishes were also received from Chesham Cricket Club and several veterans of Chesham United Football Club.

The ground was not perfect initially but in two to three years the ground became the envy of the South of England clubs. The Chairman George Barnes proposed a vote of thanks, especially

Chesham Silver Band in their full glory

to Lord Chesham: "I am very proud as Chairman of Chesham United Football Club to propose a vote of appreciation to all concerned. If I am allowed to say it, all I would like is that games should kick off at 4.00pm rather than 3.00pm."

The Chesham Town Silver Band played. Ladies sold claret and blue rosettes around the ground and a special programme was commissioned both in aid of the Club's ground equipment fund. The opening match was a 2-2 draw with Slough, The Chesham goals were in the ninth minute from Jim Ryder and F Hill in the 25th. The Slough goals in the first and last minutes of the first half by R.Morris. It was only the second point dropped by Chesham all season.

1932-33 season

The Club produced a blue fixture book for this season. Listed as the Club's Presidents were Captain the Right Honourable Lord Chesham MC and W F Lowndes Esq JP. There were also a large number of Vice Presidents, a position open to anyone donating £8.00 a season.

Chesham United 1932-1933

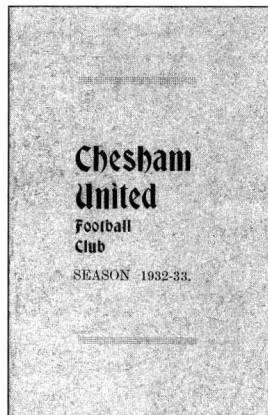

Chesham United Fixtures 1932-1933

1933-34 season

This season saw the 15th annual report of the Club's since amalgamation and the 57th year of football in Chesham. This was a season of some success in the Amateur Cup. Chesham reached the 4th round only to get an away draw at Imber Court, home of the Metropolitan Police, which they lost 4-0 after an encouraging first half. The loss was estimated at being worth £150 to the Club. The next assault was on the Berks & Bucks Cup. After games against Aylesbury and Slough, the final was played against Wycombe Wanderers at Maidenhead on Easter Monday and drawn 0-0. The replay at Reading on 5 May was won 3-0. With great hopes of the Spartan League Championship, it was a close run affair until the last few weeks of the season when Maidenhead went ahead and carried it off with a clear lead leaving Chesham running up with 37 points, the same number of points having won Chesham the championship in 1932-33.

The Club's committee had hoped for £100 from the Berks & Bucks Cup but were somewhat disappointed with only £76. Several special events were held to help balance the Club's books. One, a bazaar with assistance from local businesses, raised some £180 throughout the season.

After several attempts the Club's Honorary Secretary, Mr J G Stone, resigned due to his responsibilities with the Berks & Bucks FA after fifty years service to football in Chesham.

Several incidents took place in and around the dressing room area so on 18 February a notice, that still stands today, was posted reading "Only players and officials may enter the dressing area".

1934-35 season

This was the season Chesham hosted the Berks & Bucks semi-final on 9 March between Wycombe Wanderers and Wolverton. The more interesting events were off the field of play. The Chesham Carnival was born and the Club received the County FA's blessing for an annual 6-a-side competition of local clubs. Forty paying car park spaces were now available around the ground together with spaces for officials and away team coaches.

The contract for keeping the grass down in the close season was won by Mr Nash who duly ran sheep on the ground to keep the height of the grass manageable.

The only pitch success came with four players being selected for the Berks & Bucks; W Wheeler, J Keen, E Thorn, and D Goodson.

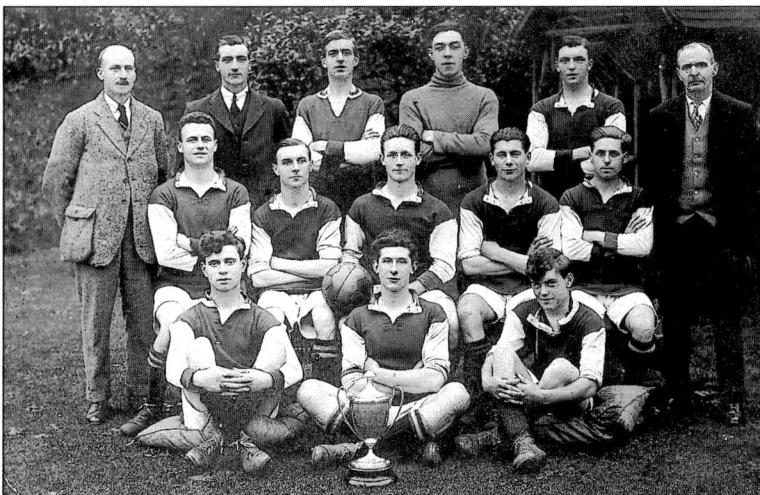

Chesham United 1934-1935

Chesham United 1937-1938

1935-36 season
Chesham finished third in the Spartan League behind Waterlows and Callender Athletic.

1936-37 season
Chesham finished eighth in the Spartan League that year.

1937-38 season
G Beach became the Spartan League's fifth highest scorer, with sixteen goals. The leading scorer was Waterlows' H Billington. These were the days of a tight line between amateur and professional players. The Chesham players were allowed the following:
a)   Railway, motor, tram, boat etc. fares or other necessary expenses actually incurred by him in travelling from and to his home or work for the purpose of playing in a match.
b)   Hotel expenses if necessary during the day and sleeping accommodation if absent for more than the day, during the actual and necessary absence from home for the purpose of playing in a match.

With only 30 goals against this season a disappointing 4th position was achieved in the league, even though some good football was played. A very healthy profit of £200 resulted in a £90 overdraft, which was some £160 less than the previous season's. County badges were won by G Keen and F Horner. Trials at Blackpool FC were given to G Keen and C Saunders. The FA invited several Chesham players on a seven week trip to USA and Canada in May and June.

1938-39 season
This was a season with little cheer, with the loss of the Club's Captain, H J Keen, in mid season not helping. H Parker took his place. C Saunders topped the goal scoring table with G Beach's 16 goals leaving him in second slot, despite his exclusion from many games because of his severe head injury sustained in the Amateur Cup tie with Worthing.

This was the season the Club hosted the Berks & Bucks Cup final for the first time between Windsor and Maidenhead. The ground was also used when the Army played Oxford University in a special. This game produced income of £13 15s 6d.

The Chesham Challenge Cup resulted in several Club donations: Chesham Cottage Hospital £5, Chalfont and Gerrards Cross Hospital £3, Berks and Bucks Benevolent Fund £1 and Chesham Nursing Association £1. The Club's season tickets were introduced of two different types, ground only and ground and stand only. A book of rules became available with 250 copies being distributed. The Club co-operated with the National Fitness Council to improve general team awareness of fitness. Training took place on the pitch, but not in goal mouths.

Discussions were under way for a merger of the Spartan and Athenian Leagues. Some fifty-three FA Cup final tickets were allocated to Chesham this season.

The car parking areas were now finished and this enabled several local clubs to use the facilities: Cestreham Athletics Club, Chesham Corinthians, Aged Mens Fellowship and the Royal Bucks Laundry who also rolled the ground for the Club. Players were all now insured through the Spartan League scheme. The first public telephone was installed, as was a bicycle stand. New arrangements had been made with Darvells the Club's caterers and Dell and Holtspur Bus Company for buses to away games. W Hawes was made a honorary life Vice-President for services of some 50 years to Chesham football. The County FA gave a green light to 11-a-side veterans' games.

1939-40 season
On 3 September 1939 war was declared with Germany. The Club's talent spotters turned to the men available. One such group were based at Latimer House, two outstanding prospects were outside right Bottrell and Wright, based with the Northants regiment. The supporters' club was disbanded for the war years and the balance of money raised, some £18, was duly presented to the Club. The ground was requisitioned by the War Office. Howard Son and Gooch acted for the Club, over-seeing all development and erection of buildings on the site. Nation-wide only 28 FA Cup matches were played.

The matches in the war years saw mainly friendly matches with Army, RAF and Navy teams. Some local company games also took place. A local Chesham team was mainly selected, firstly to keep expenses to a minimum and secondly because of the lack of players available to play.

On 27 August 1940 the ground was released by the War Office, who now allowed it to be used once more for football. The ground was kept rolled and cut. Mr J Ringsell assisted Mr G Payne on the ground.

The Chesham Sports Company, the Club's landlord asked the Club to pay any rent they could afford, as no regular gate money was being taken. The Club Directors also met with Mr Hodkinson of the Rate Collectors to discuss the Club's situation.

The Club's long standing trainer of some twenty years, Mr J Humphrey stepped down to pursue his great interest with the St John Ambulance Brigade.

1940-41 season
It was agreed by the Club's committee to join the Great Western League Combination for the 1940-41 season. The first game was at Marlow but was delayed due to an air raid. Marlow won 3-1. The first home fixture was against Windsor and Eton. The Club improved the changing rooms and enlarged the coppers. Mr C Mulkern took charge of this project, which thanks to his expertise cost only £12. The Inland Revenue asked for information on admission charges that had been set at 6d in the ground and 6d in the stand. No season tickets were produced.

1941-42 season
It was again agreed to join the Great Western League

1943

The club withdrew from the Great Western League and closed down on 12 July 1943 until hostilities ceased. Notification was sent to Chesham Sports Company.

The Club received a request from one of our chaps, Mr Grimes, for a football and also old kit for soldiers. It was agreed to send the men at the front these items.

Subscriptions were still paid to the FA and Berks & Bucks. The Club drafted a letter to Chesham Urban District Council appealing for a reduction in rates as the ground was not being used for football. The Club's heavy overdraft was causing some concern and stood at £240 3s 1d.

An agreement was made with Mr Bell, Chairman of CUDC to hold a fete to coincide with the Merchant Navy week and divide all proceeds equally between the Club and the charity. The week ran from 10 to 17 September. Major Melville asked for permission for the Home Guard Band to attend. Also suggested were side shows, children's sports, a baby show, and a tug of War. It was agreed that invitations would be sent out over a ten mile radius.

This event actually never materialised because of the time of year and the war activities. A Christmas draw was the Club's alternative method of raising funds. With rationing the prizes of poultry, spirits, wine, tobacco and cigarettes were much sought after.

1944

The Club's overdraft, which stood at £160, seems to have been the main talking point. Many ideas were proposed to reduce this. The Town's businesses that had before the war regularly hired the football ground were contacted by Eddy Greenham to see if they could assist the Club in its quest to raise funds. The company that had washed the teams' shirts for so many years, The Royal Bucks Laundry, assisted by holding a dance at the Drill Hall. A Derby sweep also seems to have been very popular.

1 July 1944 saw a co-operative fete at Botley House Garden. This was well received with many side shows that included darts, housey-housey, ninepins, a treasure hunt, Kan Kan, Bagatelle and rings. All equipment would be purchased by Mr Hobbs on a visit to London. The prizes for the fete were donated by local companies, for example whisky by Chesham Brewery Ltd.

£35 was spent on equipment. The Home Guard assisted where and when possible, even giving a £25 donation and repairing the popular stand that had been damaged. The overdraft now stood at £76.

1945

The first meeting of the Club's Committee in 1945 was on 4 April. It was announced that the ground had been relinquished by the Army Authorities. "Nissan huts would be left at the ground if the Club wanted them for a cost of £5". It was agreed to purchase one.

Post-war football had to wait for FA approval. At a meeting on Friday 4 May 1945 at Holborn the Spartan League met to restart football. Mr H Lacey and Mr J Bartlett attended for the Club. The Club was somewhat undecided which league to play in and eventually followed the likes of Slough, Windsor, and Maidenhead into the Spartan League in the Western section. This had an eighteen strong committee, rather than the twelve there were before the War.

The re-opening up of the Club's facilities bought several problems to light. The whereabouts of such things as the goal nets was discussed. They had last been used in an Inter-Police war-time game and not been put back under the stand in their regular place. The Chesham police, when approached, made a donation of some £5 towards Club funds, but didn't accept responsibility for their loss. The ground needed much work to bring it up to playable condition. Several new pieces of machinery and new tools were purchased. The goal mouths were restored at a cost of £1 10s.

Colonel Melville and the Chesham Home Guard on parade at The Meadow

Gathering of Allied Troops both U.S. and Chesham Home Guard

10 June saw the Empire Youth Parade on the ground creating much local interest. Invitations were received to enter the FA and Amateur Cup for this season and adverts placed in the Bucks Examiner, Bucks Free Press and Watford Observer for trials for new players.

In July new nets were purchased from Mr S Moreton of the Swan Inn in Old Amersham. Mr George Payne retired and a testimonial of £5 was presented to him. The first away game was against Aylesbury on Saturday 1 September 1945. Ground admission was set at 1s with 3d extra for the stand. The Chesham Sports Company's annual charge was increased in December 1945 to £100 annually. The Club was also to pay arrears of £350.

1946

The Cricket Club met with the Football Club to discuss work and general maintenance of both grounds. The Cricket Club were represented by G Newton and P Deland. Their first job was to appoint a suitable groundsman Mr Filstone. He was paid £4.10s, the Football Club paying seven twelfths and the Cricket Club the rest.

The FA asked for three stewards to attend the Cup Final between Charlton Athletic and Burnley, which Charlton won 1-0. The Club hosted the Berks and Bucks Junior cup final.

The FA wrote to all senior clubs in connection with the Bolton disaster. The Club sent a donation of £25 to the fund set up. The Club seems to have overcome its overdraft problems with a £100 credit balance being reported. The ground was used for the town's victory party.

Cambridge Town invited Chesham to a charity challenge with a hospital cup as the prize. This proved a great day out, with the Club subsequently receiving a letter of thanks and £21 expenses.

The Fire Guard training hut was purchased from the Home Guard for £1 1s.

Charles Cavendish took the chair from his father Lord Chesham after his father stood down. Edgar Rublicing paid the Club £1 to distribute the Club's fixture card. Mr C Mulkean was appointed as Club Press Secretary. For the first time Polish players were invited to play a trial match, organised on 29 August 1946 at Hodgmoor Camp, Chalfont St Giles. Three hundred copies of the Club's rules were distributed.

Len Brown became the new skipper for the 1946-7 season. Dick Goodson was appointed Manager. Match programmes were organised with a weekly income of 30s a week sold at 2d each at home matches. The FA published a book "Victory was the goal" priced at 2s 6d.

The first minuted match report was of an FA Cup tie at Oxford against Metal and Produce Recovery Dept 1 on 9 September 1946 and read as follows:

"Mr Jackman reported on the FA Cup tie at Oxford against Metal Produce Recovery Dept 1. Owing to transport difficulties, the journey was made by car. The match resulted in a draw of 1-1. The opposition were a big, strong and robust side. We faced a wind and spells of sunshine and made a shaky start being down one goal at half time. The side improved until Brown was injured, but continued to play the better football. One equaliser was scored by Meeks from a penalty given when Morgan was through but was bought down badly when within a few yards of goal. Brown was off for about twenty minutes, but we were still on top. Thomson played well, doing all that was asked of him. Meeks played his usual game, but his partner Le Ber was weak. Keen played a grand game at left half and Brown a good game until injured when he went on the wing. King was erratic. Hobbs did not seem really fit, but was satisfactory, although he has a lot to learn. Wood is a good footballer with some lovely touches. Stewart at centre forward is a real find and deputised at centre half when Brown was injured and deputised well. Morgan was definitely off colour, doubtless due to recent dental extractions. Perrie seemed nervous and did not use his speed to best effect."

The replay was arranged for Thursday September 12th and it had been arranged at Oxford that the same team play in the replay. In this replay it was decided to play in black and white. The club's reception had been good and it had been agreed with our opponents that each club should meet its own expenses for the two matches. The gate had originally been given at £4 8s but a recount gave it as £4 9s 6d. Our players' expenses were £1 8s - the cost of transport is not yet known.

Loudspeakers were introduced for announcements. A licence was taken with the Phonographic Performance Co Ltd to enable music to be played over the speaker system. New much needed shirts, pants and hose were organised, and it was hoped that clothing coupons would not be needed.

The ground was to be rolled at a cost of £1 and Mr Roberts the Club's masseur was employed at 7s 6d a session. Darvells continued serving the tea after matches but the groundsmen had to attend to the washing up. A new mower was purchased in conjunction with the Cricket Club.

Postal insurance was organised with the main stand valued at £3,000 plus £1,000 for fixtures and fittings.

1947

There was plenty of interest in the Polish Army players (Carpathians), with special interest in one back, one half-back and two forwards.

On 27 May 1947 the Club was elected to the Corinthian League. A £5 fine was levied on the Club for withdrawing from the League before 31st March. A £2 2s fine was paid under rule 6 of the League's rules. A county badge was won by A Stewart.

On 14 July 1947 the players first wore numbers on their shirts. A local tailor, Mr Hawkes, was commissioned to sew on the numbers and acquire a goalkeeper's green jersey. Mrs and Miss Hawkes were to assist and the work cost £2 2s.

Chesham War Memorial

CHAPTER 7

Corinthians Ahoy 1948-1967

1948

Mr Rance would be a torch bearer from Chesham for the Olympics held in 1948. George Terpilowski would play for Chesham if accommodation could be found, the committee was asked to assist. Mr Hare had compiled a history of football in Chesham and asked the Club to publish it. His request was turned down by the committee due to the cost.

A total ground overhaul was started, after the final home match against Windsor and Eton on 29 April 1948, which ended 1-1. Riffell Limited were appointed for the renovating work, seed was to be sown over the whole pitch and the goal mouths turfed at a cost of £25.

The Club purchased 103 tickets for England v Scotland at Wembley. It was the first Wembley appearance of England since 1938 and the game finished 1-1.

It was the first time that 14 clubs had been in the league. Chesham lost in the second round of the Memorial Shield. The highlight was the Berks & Bucks Cup final on 29 March 1948 at Reading. Chesham beat Wycombe Wanderers 2-1 before a crowd of 8,578 having defeating Maidenhead 2-1 at home and Aylesbury 4-3 away. The Junior Cup was won after beating Thatcham Town 6-5.

1948-49 season

In the Memorial Shield Chesham lost at home in the semi-final to Erith and Belvedere, who then won the final 1-0.

The chant on the terrace became:

> "Up United, up United, Chesham depends on you.
> Chesham expects that every man contributes a goal or two.
> Up United show them the way to score.
> Make the ball roll into their goal several times or more."

This was a season of many heavy defeats, but off the pitch things were better organised. A generating set was installed for lights to train under two nights a week. A healthy bank balance of £302 in credit was recorded. Toilets were installed on the popular side. Ballboys were used for the first time. Metal goal posts were purchased for £45.

The Club's loyal groundsman, G Payne, died in November 1948. A ladies team tried to take the ground for Sunday fixtures but were not allowed to.

The Club recommended several Junior players for an FA v London Schools match. These were C Baker right half, J Taylor outside right, J Norton outside left and E Morton centre half.

In the senior side players recommended for a Berks & Bucks match against the Navy were C Smith in goal, G Terpilowski, R Gilbert, L Brown, and F Hobbs. This season the Amateur Cup was played at Wembley for the first time. Bromley beat Romford 1-0. The Berks & Bucks Junior and Senior cups were won on the same weekend. Len and his brother Freddy Brown had a medal from each game.

1949-50 season

Mr Bott took over as coach, with the committee meeting weekly on a Monday evening to pick the side for the following Saturday. The first registered players forms came in the 1949-50

Chesham United 1949-1950

season. The first names on Chesham's books were C Smith, G Terpilowski, A Groves, C Baker, R Gilbert (Captain), F Biggerstaff, S Junger, G Bose, N Christophers, and J Jakubiec. It was agreed that kick off time would be at 3pm. Five players were called up to play for the league against Nigeria on 14 September 1949. After an excise visit entry to the ground was by ticket only, although children were half price. January saw the introduction of the white football. Freddie Biggerstaff had trials for Watford FC.

1950-51 season
On Easter Monday Slough were defeated in the County Cup final.

The minors or younger players up to 18 years old played on the Chesham turf for the first time as the Club started a section that was one day hoped to be a feeder into the first team.

A changed strip was worn for the first time consisting of black shorts, blue and white quartered shirts. Even a professional ball was used, the T ball being preferred over the zigzag. The year saw the introduction of the Club's crest, first on letter headings and then on the linesmen's flags. On the field Len Ling continued the Club's ties as a feeder club to Chelsea. He scored 32 goals, the League's second highest that season, being surpassed only by A King of Hounslow Town with 42 goals. L Channer was called up to Huddersfield for a trial, Frank Hobbs and Freddie Biggerstaff became county players. G Tuett played for Arsenal against Watford on 19 March in a special trial game. The team's insurance for the season was £20. The signing of Mr Hammond from St Leonards seemed to encounter difficulties. When an enquiry was made, he was found to be in hospital with a broken leg. One and a quarter hundredweights of Sutton's county mixture grass seed was spread on the ground.

1951-52 season
The main story of the season was the team's victory under George Terpilowski in the Berks & Bucks Benevolent Fund Cup. The popular stand was presented to the Club by the supporters. The first discussions about a new club house noted in the minutes. The Club's first finance committee met.

*Ron Hodgkins presents the cheque for the
popular side stand to Tommy Bartlett Club Chairman.*

*George Barnes(President), Tommy Stillman (Secretary),
Ron Hodgkins and Tommy Bartlett at the opening of the new stand.*

Chesham United 1951-1952

1952-53 season

The Club's application for entry into the Athenian League was rejected because that league had reduced by one club to fourteen. The Reading Senior Cup replaced the Wycombe Challenge Cup. Five players were invited to play for the Berks & Bucks FA against Beds FA at Wycombe. They were Darvell, Deane, Honor, Robinson, and Strain. Norman Dymock became Vice-Captain to George Terpilowski. Pre-match team sheets previously displayed at A.Bones' shop were withdrawn and teams were announced on match days because players had become confused over team selections. £19 was collected for the Lynmouth disaster fund. The Club's own appeal helped the Club break even this season., One of the Club's fund raising events was Captian Korlkoff's Cossack Riders who were paraded through the town raised £8. W Shipwright signed on as a professional for Watford in breach of FA rule 38 and was fined £11 1s. Johnny Crapper signed professional forms for Hasting United. Chesham was re-elected to the League after a poor run of results.

1953-54 season

A rock bottom season for both first and reserve teams who struggled to hold their own. In 52 games only 7 wins were achieved. Ted Beeson was appointed Coach with Alf Bone as Trainer. 650 Programmes were planned to be printed for the first team games and 250 for reserve team games. The Berks & Bucks celebrated its 75th season and 90 years of the FA. Centre half J Breeze was made Vice Captain and selected for the Corinthian League team against Trinidad at Selhurst Park. £43 was set aside for electricity to be connected. The first Blazer badges were available at 9s. A low point of this season was not only the league positions. The Christmas notes in the programme report the barracking the players had received because of their poor performances.

1954-55 season

United were just getting over a bad spell. Last season's re-election to the League was not a formality. Within the Club there were concerns that the Club's location was unfavourable.

The four concluding games of the season made good reading. They were won 6-1, 7-1, 2-1, and 8-1. Cunningham led the season's scoring with 16 followed by Dymock with 15 and Ling with 11.

1955-56 season

PC Dale of Chesham Police turns this Aylesbury shot over the bar

Chesham United's facilities were regularly used for other club and company matches. When success was limited on the field the revenue from such matches was essential to the Club's survival.

1956-57 season

Chesham lost the League Cup semi-final 1-0 to Epsom. Epsom lost the final 2-0 to Maidenhead. Maidenhead's John Reardon, subsequently Chesham's manager, scored the first goal.

1957-58 season

After two reapplications to the Corinthian League a third would have been a disaster. As an insurance against this the great step of employing a professional coach was taken. He was the Welshman Johnny Baynham, a former Brentford, Leyton Orient and Swindon winger. He improved training facilities and made fitness the team's priority.

1958-59 season

The new clubhouse, subsequently known as the Chess Suite was built. The Club was dealt a double blow with the deaths of Tommy Bartlett and Tommy Stillman. The following tribute to Tommy Stillman was noted in the Club's minutes: "It was with very deep regret that the announcement of the death of L T Stillman was recorded. His long connection with the Club started with Chesham Generals in 1907 where he was not appreciated. He moved the other end of the town and joined Chesham Town. It was incidentally in his first game against the Generals that he scored a hat trick. He represented Berks & Bucks FA (Senior) in 1913-14 and 1920-21 during the successful time with the Club. On his retirement he put all his efforts into administering the secretary's job of Chesham United. He was elected to the Berks & Bucks Council in 1949, he worked in football locally for some 50 years. Football was his number one love although he also played cricket for Chesham."

George Robinson's injury in a pre-season trial game was a big blow, as he was never able to play again this season. A couple of new faces appeared in the first game of the season against Eastbourne, they were tall Geoff Cornes, an inside forward who joined from Yiewsley and Tom Ralton, a stylish wing half from Berkhamsted Town. Several other players featured, the most prominent being George Holdford who appeared at inside forward and wing half, Johnny Gilmour an inside forward, and Mickey Ryan at wing half. Later on Keith Longman and Ken Endersby performed well as did Jimmy Morris between the sticks, with Cyril Spalding and Ken Patey both proving sound. Dave Bradshaw proved a tower of strength and determination and won "Sportsman of the Year".

The season's high came on Boxing Day afternoon, away at Uxbridge, in a game played with only 10 men for most of the time on murky, muddy day as Jimmy Norris was injured saving a penalty. Chesham completely outclassed the opposition coming out worthy winners 4-1.

Chesham United 1958-1959

1959-60 season
The league increased from 14 to 16 teams.

Jimmy Morris became the Club's "Sportsman of the Season". The award was presented by Luton's Manager Mr Sid Owen who won the National "Player of the Year" award.

The bar area of the new clubhouse that will transform the Club's finances. The bar was built by Harman Brewery of Uxbridge

Chesham United 1959-1960

1960-61 season

Chesham United 1960-1961

As the Club was turning down suggestions that the Club should turn professional, on the field the team were producing the goods. Despite having to meet players' expenses totalling £762, an increase of £168 on the previous season, a credit balance was left at a staggering £1,000. The third team was disbanded as were the Minor Team. Jimmy Morris became a county player.

1961-62 season

Chesham reached the League Cup semi-final which they lost to Edgware 4-3. They were runners up in the league for the second season. Membership was healthy at 500. Boundary fences between the cricket field and football pitch were to be improved. A fund to purchase floodlights was well under way. It was a little disappointing to miss the Amateur Cup after reaching the divisional final for the second successive year. An application to join the Athenian league was unsuccessful. The season ended with £5,000 in the bank.

Chesham United 1962-1963

1962-63 season

The Neale Trophy was won for the first time, as was the Berks and Bucks Benevolent Cup. The Corinthian League Memorial Shield was also won. Chesham United joined the Athenian League at the end of the season. The season's player of the year was Johnny Willis and soccer ace Jimmy Greaves presented him with the trophy. On 18 January 1963 Chesham's match with Corinthian Casuals, which had been postponed several times because of the bad winter weather, was eventually played at the Oval Cricket Ground, Kennington. This was the last ever football match played at the ground and was won by Chesham.

1963-64 season

The Club entered the Athenian League Division One. The Club's reserves were runners up to Letchworth Town. The final game of the season was the Berks & Bucks Benevolent Cup and it marked a fine individual achievement and a new club scoring record, possibly never to be beaten. The Club's Footballer of the Year, Johnny Willis, scored 50 goals in the season.

Mr George Hawes, Chesham's President since 1957 died aged 69. He was a Director of W Hawes Ltd, the Brush Manufacturers. The celebrations for 100 years of the FA was attended by Ron Hodkins, the Club Secretary.

Chesham United 1963-1964 League Runners-up

1964-65 season

The Club's most important project to date was the introduction of floodlights. A special match against Luton Town managed by Sid Owen was organised. A very young Bruce Rioch was in their starting line up. Through much local company support and funds raised by the supporters' club, the floodlights were purchased at a cost of £4,500. Special cables were laid by the Eastern Electricity Board. The switch on was performed by Mr D Follows MBE (Secretary of the FA) on 22 September 1964.

The 1964 Chesham United Committee

Spec the Examiner's Editor since 1924 passed away in May 1964. No CUFC history would be complete without a short mention of his contributions in the Bucks Examiner each week. He was a life long follower of football in Chesham, who gave the Club more than its fair share of coverage over the years.

The Berks and Bucks Senior Cup was bought home after a 4-2 defeat of Slough Town on 19 April. The players were treated to a Club tour to Amsterdam on 14 June.

1965-66 season

England's World Cup victory didn't seem to inspire Chesham. A season of 60 games was played. The opening match of the season against Aylesbury at home was won 3-2. On 4 September was an FA Cup away game at Banbury which Chesham lost 2-0. Chesham fared better in the Amateur Cup, winning 2-1 at home against Vauxhall Motors, and 2-0 at home against Letchworth. A 1-1 draw at Tring was followed by a home win at the replay of 4-2. A defeat of 3-1 away was inflicted by Hemel Hempstead in early November. In the league a good Christmas period with home wins of 7-3 over Wokingham and 5-0 against Wembley and a 6-1 away victory at Harrow was not enough to pull Chesham higher than 6th position for the season.

Chesham United 1965-1966

1966-67 season

The season opened with a game against Erith and Belvedere away being drawn 2-2. The first Sunday league matches were played. Ex-Chesham player Stewart Morse played for Wales in an International Amateur match against Ireland scoring both goals in the 2-1 win. The John Hearn Cup was won in a 5-1 victory over Amersham. New manager John Reardon was appointed on 21 April. Terry Reardon and Johnny Willis played at both county and national level this season.

The season's highlight was the winning of the Berks & Bucks Senior Cup. The campaign started with an extra time win of 2-1 against Slough. The semi-final against Maidenhead was won 2-1 with Dennis Wells in goal for Maidenhead. On Easter Monday, 27 March at Maidenhead against old rivals Wycombe Wanderers it was an extra time goal by J Cooley in the 95th minute that gave a famous victory to the underdogs. John Pyatt left the club to join Liverpool.

Chesham United 1966-1967 – Winners of the Berks & Bucks Senior Cup Final
L Chittenden, S Prosser, M Scott, C Goodough, J Cooley, A Binfield, B Dunton
B Caterer, A Appleby, J Willis, B Gogan, J Harter, L Burgess, M McCaffrey

Programme for Enfield v Chesham 20th November 1966

CHAPTER 8

Wembley Here We Come! 1967-1968

This was Chesham United's best season ever. Several of the Club's original 1919 team made the trip to Wembley. Cyril Webb, who was 78, recalled the first season's excitement and the trill of being the Club's first skipper. In 1919 Chesham were a feared side. He felt that Dennis Wells was the greatest asset the club possessed.

The John Hearn Cup was retained with a 4-0 win over Amersham. The supporters donated a silver cup and a presentation book to honour the Club's Wembley visit. The Club's annual dinner held at the end of the season was attended by 300 people and Captain Les Burgess received the Sportsman of the Year award for the whole team. The Bucks Examiner presented a clock for the main stand.

Memories of Wembley 1968

In the football almanac for the season 1966-67 a message reads "a tip for next season is a little town in the Buckinghamshire countryside will get to Wembley". No truer word could have been written.

Brian Caterer had just returned from watching the Amateur Cup Final. He turned to his pal and said "Next season we will be here at Wembley."

I was very lucky to be able to interview Brian in Maidenhead and record his recollections of thirty years ago. Chesham started with odds of 1,000 to 1 on their winning the Amateur Cup. Curiously the winner of the Grand National that year came in at those odds. Brian was only 24 years old. Born in Hayes on 23 January 1943, Brian's passage to Chesham was a rocky one. With an illegal approach being made for him, a 6 week suspension had been imposed on him before he could play. He played at centre back alongside team captain Les Burgess.

He unfolded in a tale of immense happiness and despite the passage of time his memories are still crystal clear.

The build up to the final had seen the team train on mature, spongy turf at Ley Hill Golf Club. Certain adaptations in play were necessary with the Chesham pitch 5 yards wider than Wembley's. The pressure was looming in the league with 14 games to be played in the last 7 weeks of the season. Leading up to the final Chesham won no games, drawing four and losing five.

Fitness was a key factor and curiously the Slough Rugby Captain Ian Bundey devised a series of circuit training programmes to help to bring the team to peak fitness. They were possibly the fittest team in the South. Other local help came from Ken Furphy, the Watford Manager, who allowed all the injured players to receive free treatment. The main final worries apart from Brian were Dave Ellis and Mick McCaffrey who both had pain killing injections before kick off. Brian recollects the normal match fee being £6 a week but a special bonus of £20 for the final appearance.

The kick-off at 3pm on Saturday 20 April 1968 signalled some last minutes crises. Special Wembley trains left Chesham at 11.15, 1.08 and 1.38 at 7s return, stopping at Chalfont & Latimer, Chorleywood and Rickmansworth. But where was Diane Caterer's ticket? She had left it on the kitchen table. Fortunately, an FA official from Hayes managed to get her into the match.

Of the 54,000 crowd, 14,000 came from Chesham with 6,000 from Amersham and some 60 coaches left the Meadow.

CHESHAM UNITED'S
RECORD BREAKING
F.A. AMATEUR CUP-RUN
1967 – 68

Date		Round	Match	Ven.	Score	Scorers	Att.
Sept	23	Preliminary	H. Hempstead	(A)	2 - 0	Fruen, Black	550
Oct.	7	1st Qual.	Didcot	(H)	3 - 0	Ellis (2), Fruen	700
	21	2nd Qual.	Hazells	(A)	2 - 0	Ellis, Goode	500
Nov.	4	3rd Qual.	Marlow	(H)	3 - 1	Fruen, McCaffrey	750
Dec.	16	4th Qual.	Soham	(A)	1 - 1	Fruen	250
	23	4th Qual. (Replay)	Soham	(H)	1 - 0	Burgess	1,000
Jan.	20	1st Proper	Maidenhead	(H)	2 - 2	Fruen, Harper	1,000
	27	1st (Replay)	Maidenhead	(A)	2 - 2	Ellis, Harper	800
	31	1st (2nd Replay)	Maidenhead	(N)	2 - 1	Harper, Black	1,750
Feb.	3	2nd Round	Dulwich H.	(A)	1 - 1	Fruen	1,100
	10	2nd (Replay)	Dulwich H.	(H)	4 - 2	Fruen, Harper (2) Frost	1,200
	17	3rd Round	Corinthian-C.	(A)	0 - 0		1,250
	24	3rd (Replay)	Corinthian-C.	(H)	1 - 0	Fruen	1,400
Mar.	2	4th Round	Oxford City	(A)	0 - 0		3,500
	9	4th (Replay)	Oxford City	(H)	2 - 0	Ellis, Frost	4,150
	16	Semi-Final	Wealdstone	(N)	2 - 0	Fruen, Ellis	8,500

Played—16 Goals for—28 Against—10

Official total playing time 24 hours 30 minutes.

CHESHAM UNITED
FOOTBALL CLUB
FOUNDED 1919

MEMBERS OF THE FOOTBALL ASSOCIATION
BERKS & BUCKS F.A.   —   ATHENIAN LEAGUE
PREMIER MID-WEEK FLOODLIGHT LEAGUE

OFFICIAL PROGRAMME
PRICE 6d.   SEASON 1967/68

LUCKY

10/- voucher will be issued to Lucky No. winner.
The voucher must be spent with an advertiser in the programme.

*Programme for the 4th Round Replay
against Oxford City*

FA AMATEUR CUP RUN 1968

PROGRAMME COVERS

F.A.
AMATEUR
CUP

SOUVENIR
PROGRAMME
1/-

SEMI-FINAL TIE
CHESHAM UNITED v WEALDSTONE
AT CRAVEN COTTAGE S.W.6.
SATURDAY 16th MARCH 1968 Kick off 3.0. p.m.

*Programme for the semi-final tie
against Wealdstone*

There was real cup fever around Chesham with many shop window decked out in claret and blue. A song was written and sung. George Tutil presented a special flag to be flown at Wembley. The only disappointment was the fact that Ted Woodward and Louis Stalder, local sports outfitters, had put black numbers on the all white kit to be worn on the special day instead of claret numbers. Leytonstone won the toss and wore their home strip.

The Chesham camera club filmed the semi-final and final action. Brian reflects on the penalty miss and the disappointment of losing but it is a memory that lives with him daily. "The ordeal of walking out in front of some 50,000 people certainly sent a cold shiver down my spine. To say I was nervous was a understatement. I was terrified. I had barely slept for three nights just

Field-Marshal Montgomery of Alamein greeting the Chesham Team

John Reardon leads out his team for the Cup Final

Chesham on the attack during the Final

thinking about 3.00pm on Saturday. Our blazers were all new and Lawrence supplied us with new boots and sports bags. I wasn't so keen on Lawrence's boots so I painted on my Puma boot the same design so no one would know".

Les Burgess, Chesham United's captain, greets the Leytonstone captain, Alan Minall

"We all spent the night before the final at home not at a fancy hotel and met as usual for the coach. The bus driver took a wrong turn and we entered Wembley through a back entrance, but the ovation we received getting through Wembley Way was breathtaking, clapping, cheering, flags flying, horns going off."

"We had the England dressing room (the north dressing room). We all had an individual bath and a large communal bath, showers in plenty, pipes heated the floor. We were all very proud. Many people called us country bumpkins but we had a lot of pride in Bucks. There were three thousand people who welcomed Chesham on their return from Wembley, whereas the winners Leytonstone were only welcomed by 90 people."

"£3,000 ticket money taken by Chesham the day before the final couldn't be kept at Chesham police station so police inspector Charles Peett took the money home for safe keeping."

Chesham United's players receiving their runners-up medals from Field-Marshal Montgomery

The season

72 games were played that season including 28 cup games. The result of the Club's first game, a 4-3 home win over Bletchley, gave a taste of things to come. It was followed by two games also at home drawn 1-1 with Harlow and 0-0 with Edgware. It wasn't until 23 September away at Hemel Hempstead that the touch paper was lit. The attendance at this FA Amateur Cup preliminary round match was 550. Chesham won 2-0.

The next obstacle was the second qualifying round match, a home game with Didcot Town on Saturday 7 October, which was won 3-0 before 700 spectators.

The third qualifying round was at home against Marlow. The game was won 3-1, with attendance of 750.

On Saturday 16 December 1967 the fourth qualifying round was played away against Soham United, an East Anglian side, and drawn 1-1 before 250. The replay on Saturday 23 December 1967 was won at home 1-0 with 1,000 in attendance.

Chesham then played Maidenhead in the first round proper. The first encounter on Saturday 20 January 1968 was a 2-2 draw at home. The replay a week later away was also a 2-2 draw. The second replay took place on Wednesday 31 January 1968 at Loakes Park High Wycombe. Dave Ellis had a night to remember when he missed a penalty and later on an open goal. Joe Harper had opened the scoring for Chesham before Maidenhead equalised. As the game progressed a third draw seemed on the cards but with only ten seconds left on the watch, Dave Black dumped Maidenhead out of the Cup in a most dramatic way and Chesham won 2-1.

The second round was played away against Dulwich Hamlet on Saturday 3 February 1968 and drawn 1-1. Chesham took an early lead, but conceded a penalty to Dulwich's captain three minutes from time.

The replay took place on the following Saturday at home and Chesham took the opportunity of increasing admission prices. The gate was 1,200, so obviously the local crowd still found the Club's play value for money, especially as they won 4-2.

Chesham seemed determined to play every round twice over as they next drew the third round 0-0 away against Corinthian Casuals a week later. A further week onwards they won 1-0 at home in the replay.

On Saturday 2 March 1968, the form continued in the quarter-final away against Oxford City, where a crowd of 3,482, saw the teams draw 0-0. Saturday 9 March saw the replay at home was won 2-0 before 4,100. It says much for Chesham's determination that they had won through despite playing and replaying such crucial games at weekly intervals.

The semi-final on Saturday 16 March was on neutral ground. Attended by 8,500, the match at Craven Cottage saw United crush Wealdstone 2-0 on their way to the final at Wembley.

THE FOOTBALL ASSOCIATION
AMATEUR CUP COMPETITION

FINAL

Chesham United

versus

Leytonstone

SATURDAY 20th APRIL 1968
Kick-off 3 p.m.

WEMBLEY
EMPIRE STADIUM

**The Amateur Cup Final at 3.00pm on Saturday 20 April 1968
at Wembley Stadium - Chesham United v Leytonstone.**

The match attendance was 52,000. The guest of honour was Field Marshall the Right Honourable Viscount Montgomery of Alamein KG,GEB,DSO.

The running order for the day was:

1.45 - 2.50	The Royal Artillery Band,
	The Royal Artillery Slow March.
1.	March Medley, Sousa On Parade
2.	Tune of the Day from Fiddler on the Roof.
3.	Waltz Medley, The Gay Nineties
4.	Descriptive Cranberry Corners USA
5.	Excerpts from the Sound of Music
6.	Sing with Ken Dodd
7.	Two pieces La Golondrina, Spanish gypsy dance
8.	TV March Thunderbirds.

The final itself was overshadowed by the early injuries to Leytonstone's players, Bobby Hammes and John Albon, who was carried off with a broken leg in the 17th minute. Leytonstone's goal in the 69th minute coupled with Kenny Kent's missed penalty in the second half proved decisive. The final score of 1-0 in Leytonstone's favour does not really reflect the balance of effort that had been put in by the two sides in reaching Wembley and Chesham's ultimate failure to win the trophy should not diminish the respect that should rightly be accorded to the team for the stamina and skill they had demonstrated on their way through competition, which involved over twenty four hours on the field.

A view from the bench

Another player's view of the season came from Steve Bates, who played in Chesham United Reserves in the 1967-68 season:

"Chesham United's best ever season culminated with the first ever Wembley experience for the Club. During the season the First Team were ably supported by a strong Reserve XI which supplied three players for the final team.

A run of 18 unbeaten games between October 1967 and January 1968 was one of the most successful for years. The three players who progressed to the first team were, goalkeeper Dennis Wells who took over from the injured Alan Binfield towards the end of the cup run and held his place with some excellent performances. Forward, or as described in those days inside left, Joe Harper was young skilful player who was the player involved in the penalty awarded to Chesham at Wembley. "Supersub" Peter Frost played an important role in the Cup run but to my memory didn't get onto the field at Wembley.

Other players from the reserve side managed by Johnny Gilmour were: Dave Neale Full Back, Steve Parker Full Back, Dave Jones Central Defender, Bob Hooper Defender, Gerry Olsen Centre Half, Starky Bowden Midfield, Steve Bates Midfield, Algy Baldwin Midfield, Mick Dwight Midfield, George Goode Striker, Johnny Gilmour Player Manager, Derek Jarmin Winger, and Geoff Hammond Winger. Several of this team were later to play for the First XI in the season that followed."

Steve also recollected a number of other players who made good: "First there was Kerry Dixon. He was the son of a Luton team player and played with the then current Chesham manager Brendan McNally. Kerry played for Chesham for a few months following his departure from Luton. He soon moved to Reading, Chelsea and England and became a well known First Division star. I can recall a training session at the meadow when a young Dixon was paired with me for ball exercises and how I subsequently offered him advice on one touch passing. Little did I know what effect I was to have on this youngster's future career!

Then there was Stewart Scullion, who came to Chesham in the early 60's with two other players from the Heathrow area, Alan Freeman and Brian Farr who joined the club with Scullion when Johnny Baynham was Manager. They all played in Chesham United's youth team in the FA Youth Cup. Pioneer Scouts always provided the nucleus of the side and the three players increased the strength of the team. Scullion eventually left Chesham after starring in the first team on the right wing. He signed professional terms for Charlton Athletic before becoming a well known player for Watford and Sheffield United. A goal scored for Watford against Manchester United at Old Trafford is still rated by Stewart as one of the best he scored."

"Although I only see Chesham play a few times each season I can still remember the first game I watched at the age of 6. Chesham lost at home to Maidstone United 0-5. It was the beginning of a long relationship with the Club as a supporter, helper to the groundsman Norman Richardson and eventually a player. There are several players who over the years made a lasting impression. Jimmy Morris the goalkeeper of the 1950's, Cyril Spalding who took us lads for training and always made us use the cold shower after the bath, Les Patterson whose penalty kicks were the best I have ever seen, Arthur Howlett needs no introduction and Les Burgess for the way he turned up for matches and training (pin striped suit and bowler hat), Micky Scott for being one of the toughest midfielders and Brian Caterer for being the most ruthless tacklers I can remember. He always smiled at players as he helped them to their feet afterwards."

Chesham United's Wembley heroes 1968

CHAPTER 9

Times of Stagnation 1968-1983

1968-69 season

After the success of the previous season, stability was paramount for the Club. This proved impossible, many players being unsettled by offers from other clubs. The pillar and captain at the back, Les Burgess, had impressed Wealdstone in the Cup semi-final of the previous season and he joined them. Eddie Gibbins, the Hayes manager signed Caterer, Faven, Harper and Ellis. Harper later rejoined Chesham. The ex-Wycombe trainer Doug Cubbage joined from Reading.

The first game of the season saw Chesham at home to newly promoted Lewes. The game was drawn 1-1, with Chesham fielding a team unfamiliar with each other of Wells, Thackery, Smith, McCafferey, Olson, Eyres, Sargent, Black, Ball, Reardon and Willis.

Some benefits did result from the previous season's success. An invitation match was played against the Beds FA for the Ansell Cup. The result was a 0-0 draw, Beds won on a coin toss. Automatic entry to the first round proper in the FA Cup was assured with an away tie at Colchester United. This was lost 5-0, before a 5,497 gate with ex-Spurs winger Terry Dyson causing the damage. Losing 2-0 at home in the early rounds of the Amateur Cup to Walthamstow was a disappointment, but the team did win the Memorial Shield 4-3 against Aylesbury. Derek Smith was picked for the Berks & Bucks side. Brian Thackery was voted "Sportsman of the Year". High Club expectations lead on 28 February 1969 to John Reardon's departure, with Barry Darvill taking over as Manager.

1969-70 season

A very heavy, 5-0 defeat by Hitchin in the FA Cup and a 3-2 loss before 1,350 to Slough in the Amateur Cup with Kenny Kent, Chesham's erstwhile Amateur Cup penalty misser, scoring the winning goal, were the chief lowlights of the season. The season's highlight was the reserve section's success in coming league runners up.

1970-71 season

Whilst the reserve section were receiving all the accolades for their success in the Autumn and the Spring sections, the first team were really struggling. Several projects were instituted, with a new 200 club to bolster funds and the fireworks on 5 November as important off field fund raisers. £100 was spent on fireworks. Steve Bates was picked for the Berks & Bucks. On 13 November Barry Darvill was sacked for poor results. The new manager was Brendan McNally who joined on 21 November. He played in the Luton FA Cup Final team of 1959, which was lost 2-1 to Nottingham Forest and had won 4 Eire caps against Czechoslovakia, Romania, Iceland and Scotland.

1971-72 season

The Club's committee discussed at some length running a team in the Premier Midweek floodlit league. The Club had also in the last two years run a darts team that had come runners up and winners of the Chesham District League.

Membership was running at 300 with 15 associate members. The season's first win was away at Hazel Sports 5-1 with a Bobby Harper hat trick. A new strip was unveiled. Still claret and blue, there was instead of a plain jersey a slightly different design with claret shorts and blue hooped socks instead of white shorts and socks.

First team players were advised to stop playing Sunday football due to injuries. On 31 October Len Worley ex-England non-league International made his debut. Geoff Weeks and Dennis Wells were selected for the Berks & Bucks FA. A tour of Denmark was planned to visit ex-Chesham player, now manager, Jimmy Strain. The supporters held a minute's silence on the death of stalwart Frank Pearce. A six-a-side trophy was purchased in his memory.

1972-73 season
Leo Chittenden resigned as Club President. The Club's bar could only open before and after matches by law. This was the Club's last season in the Athenian League, Chesham being invited with 15 other clubs to join the Isthmian League.

Kenny Bevan was picked for Berks & Bucks. The Berks & Bucks final was played at Chesham on 23 April. The Meadow hosted the first ladies floodlit match between Amersham Angels and QPR.

1973-74 season
Pre-season friendlies included the Danish champions Aarhus AFI880, managed by ex-Chesham player Jimmy Strain. Chesham joined the Isthmian League Division II, receiving in this season £427 from league sponsors Rothmans. An anonymous donation of the same figure helped club funds. The league was to be increased to 18 clubs for the new season. 10,000 Bingo tickets had been sold over the last 7 years to support the Club, but the supporters club's membership had declined to only 200. This would be the last season of the Amateur Cup and the reserves played their first ever Sunday game against Marlow.

1974-75 season
The Club's lack of helpers prompted calls that the Club should be disbanded. The Club's funds were boosted by hosting the year's Berks & Bucks Senior Cup final between Thatcham and Wycombe Wanderers. Striker Stewart Atkins became the Club's first professional player followed in the same season by Gary Titterton and Ken Gregory. Philip Sewell was picked for the Berks & Bucks and Mr A Stone was elected a Life President.

1975-76 season
The Meadow was used to follow the fortunes of Brenton United in the TV serial Striker. Chesham reached fourth place in the league but conceded too many goals . Pre-season saw the signing of the ex-Wimbledon player, Eddie Bailham. Apart from a fire in the dressing room late on 30 March, and the season's heaviest defeat of 6-0 at Harwich and Parkeston the season was a success. Old boy Jimmy Strain bought the club he was managing in Denmark, Boldludden Frem FC, over to Chesham on tour, and the Berks & Bucks Senior Cup was won for the first time in a decade.

The Berks & Bucks competition started with a replayed game with Windsor and Eton and a super 2-0 away defeat of Maidenhead. In the semi-final against Wycombe Wanderers, Wycombe played Graham McKenzie who had already played in the tournament for Hungerford when on loan there. One of the most exciting games saw Wycombe winning 4-2, although unluckily Ken Gregory broke his leg. A protest was lodged and Chesham replaced Wycombe in the final. Hungerford were Chesham's opponents with this match played at Slough. Chesham won with a fine 4-0 score.

Stewart Atkins was the league's highest scorer with 34 goals and fourth highest in all this season's seven non-league leagues.

1976-77 season

As Brendan McNally was in hospital, Derek Smith took over the Manager's job. Chesham's FA Cup run was ended by Brentford. Having disposed of Tring 3-0 with two goals from Alan Cordice and one from Stewart Atkins, the team beat Thame 3-0 away. Banbury Town were defeated on their home ground with two further goals from Alan Cordice and one from Stewart Atkins being rounded off with an own goal. The home game against Worcester City in the fourth qualifying round was won 4-2, giving Worcester their first defeat in seventeen games. Atkins,

Chesham United 1976-1977

Programme for the 1st round FA Cup match against Brentford

Beavon, Faulkner and Marshall were the scorers. Brentford managed by former Fulham and Northampton star Bill Dodgin, with stars like Roger Cross and John Fraser, an ex-Fulham player in the 1975 FA Cup Final were always going to be a tough task. At Griffin Park Chesham eventually lost 2-0 to goals from Roger Cross and Mickey French, in front of a 2,000 crowd. A good luck letter was sent by Worcester City to Chesham. The next Saturday in the FA Trophy away at Waterlooville, Chesham were well beaten 5-0. Chesham finished the season without a booking or a send off.

1977-78 season

The season began with the Isthmian league being re-numbered. Chesham were now in Division One. 12 clubs were competing in the league. New signings were Lawrence Coyne, a cultured full back ex-Cambridge United, Johnny Morris, a midfield player once with Boreham Wood and St Albans, and a young 16 year old making his name, Kerry Dixon.

The league unveiled new incentives for goal scoring with a £208 bonus sponsored by Radio Luxembourg. A fall over cup final from the previous season had to be played against Banbury Town in the Shaw & Kilburn Cup which Chesham won on a two leg aggregate 3-1. A 9-0 win over Witney Town still failed to deflect criticism from Manager McNally and his 8 year reign ended with Mike Hall the ex-Marlow and Maidenhead boss taking over.

The season's other high points were the Berks & Bucks Cup semi-final which was lost 3-1 to Wycombe Wanderers, and meeting Finchley five times in League and Cup matches.

1978-79 season

Mike Hall appointed an assistant Peter Wright. The opening game against Bishop Stortford ended in a 2-1 defeat and the season continued unsuccessfully. The question of the Youth Team was discussed, but lack of space through the running of a reserve team, meant the option was not taken up. Club subscriptions rose from 50p to £1 a season.

1979-80 season

The Club's best FA Cup run was in this season. In the first qualifying round they beat Boreham Wood 2-0 at home. Support was at a low ebb with gate receipts of only £80.

In the next round they beat Haverhill Rovers 3-0 in the home replay after a 0-0 away draw. Chesham's Amateur Cup form of draws followed by a win on the replay, seemed to back, for in the next round they beat Bedford Town 1-0 away after a 0-0 home draw.

Maidstone United became the first team to score against Chesham in the Cup, but were completely outplayed in this 3-1 home victory. Then came the first round proper, which saw Chesham defeat Minehead 2-1 away. In the second round a home draw of 1-1 with Merthyr Tydfil was followed by a 3-1 win away on the replay. Saturday 5 January 1980 saw the FA Cup 3rd round match against Cambridge United. Chesham's glorious FA Cup run came to an end after some 10 matches. The match was played before the Club's record gate of 5,000. Cambridge's goals came from Roger Gibbins in the 30th minute, and from the record signing George Reilly in the 78th and Chesham fell out of the competition defeated 2-0. The details of the Cup Run were as follows:

First Qualifying Round

CHESHAM UNITED (0) 2 BOREHAM WOOD (0) 0
Chesham bounced back from an FA Trophy defeat at Wellingborough the week before to upset

Isthmian Premier Division Boreham Wood in a stormy match that saw three Wood players booked and manager Micky Lennon and striker Mick Jackson sent off. United — without Rene Glenister, Chris Nash and Norman Dodd — won with second half goals from Danny Johnson and Rob Martell, Martell's a spectacular effort from a seemingly impossible angle. In comparison to today's money-spinner, gate receipts were just £80.

Second Qualifying Round

HAVERHILL ROVERS (0) 0 CHESHAM UNITED (0) 0
 Chesham had probably the bigger share of the chances in a closely-fought battle with Town and Country League champions Haverhill, including a powerful header from Norman Dodd that bounced on the line and over the bar, but were relieved to live another day.

Second Qualifying Round Replay

CHESHAM UNITED (1) 3 HAVERHILL ROVERS (0) 0
Danny Johnson gave Chesham a 1-0 half-time lead and then Norman Dodd with a header and a full-blooded 30 yarder from Tim Smith in the space of three minutes saw United in to the next round.

Third Qualifying Round

CHESHAM UNITED (0) 0   BEDFORD TOWN (0) 0
Chesham players have said since that the two matches against Southern League Bedford were their toughest hurdles in the Cup run and in the first match at The Meadow, they undoubtedly came closest to losing. Tim Smith had to head two chances off the line in an exciting match and Rob Martell will still have nightmares about how he failed to score 10 minutes from time with only goalkeeper Peter Walters to beat.

Third Qualifying Round Replay

BEDFORD TOWN (0) 0 CHESHAM UNITED (0) 1
Arguably the turning point in the Cup run. Chesham battled every inch of the way in a tense, pulsating match with Rene Glenister unlucky not to score for Chesham with a stunning 30-yard shot against the bar in the first half. Danny Johnson finally settled the tie 15 minutes from the end with a penalty after Glenister had been tripped and Chesham, with goalkeeper Billy Barber in brilliant form, gave a mature and professional performance to hang on for victory. Also in top form was Chris Nash, at his best in what was to be his last game for the club.

Fourth Qualifying Round

CHESHAM UNITED (1) 3 MAIDSTONE UNITED (0) 1
Maidstone—who gave Second Division Charlton such a fright in the Third Round last season —were completely outplayed, even though they became the first team to score against Chesham in the Cup. But by the time Dave Wiltshire had headed Maidstone's goal in the 58th minute, Chesham were already two up through Rob Martell in the first half and Danny Johnson three minutes into the second half. Steve Woolfrey, playing only his second full first-team match of

the season wrapped it up in the 62nd minute to put Chesham into the First Round Proper for the fourth time in their history.

First Round Proper

MINEHEAD (1) 1 CHESHAM UNITED (1) 2

Having failed to pull a League club out of the draw, Chesham viewed the long trip to Somerset with some trepidation but after falling a goal behind they tore Southern League Minehead apart in the second half to reach the Second Round for the first time ever. Bobby Horrastead, back in the side for Rene Glenister, hit the underside of the bar in the fifth minute and then Minehead player-manager Willie Brown punished a defensive error to put his side in front after 20 minutes. But Steve Woolfrey scored Chesham's first-ever goal in the First Round when he lunged forward in the 38th minute to head home after Alan Jackett's lob had hit the bar.   Norman Dodd headed Chesham's winner from John Watt's 61st minute corner and from then on Chesham dominated the match to secure a famous victory and the perfect 25th birthday present for captain John Watt.

The 1979-1980 side which reached the 3rd Round of the FA Cup

Second Round

CHESHAM UNITED (0) 1 MERTHYR TYDFlL (1) 1

Chesham and their Welsh Southern League visitors made up for having the match postponed due to a waterlogged pitch with a thrilling battle in front of the biggest Meadow crowd for years—3,052. With first-choice keeper Billy Barber on holiday in Australia, 19-year-old reserve Martin Baguley was thrown in at the deep end after bids to sign League goalkeepers — including former Arsenal keeper Bob Wilson — had failed. Baguley played brilliantly as Chesham fought back from an unfortunate penalty in the 22nd minute with a storming second half performance that brought an equaliser in the 52nd minute from Steve Woolfrey. Chesham's assistant manager Peter Wright called the match '-a tremendous advert for non-League football.

Second Round Replay

MERTHYR TYDFIL (1) 1 CHESHAM UNITED (1) 3
Real Roy of the Rovers stuff this one. Chesham arrived at Merthyr's icy bone-hard pitch without suitable footwear but a hurried shopping spree before the game and another one just before the second half for Danny Johnson paid dividends as United pulled back from a goal down to win 3-1 in front of a crowd of 4.500. With Chesham struggling to keep their grip, Derek Elliott put Merthyr ahead after 15 minutes but the Isthmian Leaguers equalised four **minutes later** when Merthyr player-manager Doug Rosser turned Danny Johnson's cross into his own net. Chesham took command in the second half and Johnson capped a brilliant game by laying on the winning goals within a minute of each other nine minutes from time for Bobby Horrastead and John Watt.

1980-81 season
New shirt sponsors were introduced. They were Kemble Organ Sales (Yamaha) and new track suits were supplied by M6 Papers of Macclesfield. New signings were Dave Woodbridge, Ralph Perna, Seamus Byrne, Gary Hyams, and Steve Green. Pre-season games commenced with a 4-0 home win over Reading. Watford were also played. The Dave Timberlake Trophy was won with a 3-1 defeat of Holmer Green. But Holmer Green took revenge in the Berks & Bucks Senior Cup by beating Chesham 3-1 at the Meadow. They went on to lose to Milton Keynes in the semi-final.

The Club bid a sad farewell to the scorer of United's first ever goal, Sid Gomm who died in February. They also mourned the death of goal keeper Billy Barber, who took his own life after a dispute with a girlfriend.

The Club bounced back in a thrilling home match against Lewes which was won 6-4. The youth side won the Berks & Bucks Youth Cup on 3 April 3-2 against Slough at Marlow.

Chesham United 1980-1981

1981-82 season
At a public meeting on 11 January some 60 supporters were faced with the question of whether it was worthwhile continuing as a football club, and the question of Chesham Rugby Club

taking over the facilities was discussed. At a extraordinary meeting a target of £2,500 needed to be raised to save the Club and the Bucks Examiner set up a campaign to secure the Club's future. By early February the same year £450 had been donated by local businesses, and every house in the Town had been leafleted, donations being sent to the treasurer Richard Wyatt.

Mick Taylor took over on 15 January as Manager. The season came to an end when Barking knocked Chesham out 1-0 with a superb display by young Kevin Hitchcock later to star for Chelsea. A 5-4 win at Lewes kept United up. With this winter's freezing weather the dressing room boiler packed up. Woodley and Hart provided a new one free of charge with AM Mechanical Services connecting up the new boiler for nothing.

1982-83 season

20 November's FA Cup first round match home to Yeovil should have been a classic but the 1-0 defeat was marred by crowd trouble and Yeovil's goal after nine minutes sealed Chesham's fate. The FA Cup run had started back in September with a 3-2 win over Cray Wanderers, with two goals by Husley and one by Adams. Another home tie in the second qualifying round saw a win 3-1 over Clapton with goals from Nash, Thorn and Morrissey. Feltham in the third qualifying round resulted in a fine 1-0 win, Steve Adams again on the scorer. A seemingly tough away tie at Chelmsford City proved a waltz in a 3-1 win with goals from Morrissey and Husley, who scored twice. An appearance for Doncaster Rovers against Hull City by Steve Adams put the player and Club in deep water with the FA. Adams continued to play the season for Chesham.

The Great Fire of 1983

The fire destroyed 63 years of Meadow memories. The 1982-83 season was placed in turmoil when on the evening of 3 May 1983 the main stand was set alight by an electrical fault. The Club's semi-final with Hemel Hempstead in the St Mary's Cup had just finished, Hemel winning 4-3. As supporters looked on, the blaze took hold and within five minutes the old stand was totally destroyed. The remaining fixture with Boreham Wood was played on the playing field at Chalfont St Peter. A previously organised friendly with Hyde United on 16 May did take place even though there were no changing facilities available. Desperately needed funds were raised. The Club were under insured with only £45,000 of cover. Initial quotes ranged from £75,000 to £250,000 for the building of a modern stand.

The great fire on 3 May 1983 and its aftermath

CHAPTER 10

Spark to Fame 1983-1993

1983-84 season

Two weeks before the start of the 1983-84 season work began on the new stand. The tough Isthmian League ground grading rules had to be followed. An appeal was set up called "Help Chesham Stand Up". This appeal raised £10,000 and helped bridge the gap between the amount needed and the insurance money. Home games were played at Tring Town, Slough Town, Hemel Hempstead, Hayes, Aylesbury, Clapton, and Hertford Town.

The first home fixture was against Hitchin Town in the FA Cup 3rd qualifying round. The Cricket Club was used for changing. Unfortunately Hitchin won 2-0. The first league fixture was on 8 February against Feltham FC who were bottom of the league. Chesham won 3-0, and the season finished brightly considering the conditions. After the Boxing Day win over Oxford City, Chesham were top of the League.

At Chesham United's AGM held on 4 July 1983 it had been revealed that the Club had an financial loss for the year. It was in the region of £14,000, an unfortunate record loss. The main reason was the fire, although the committee stated that sweeping ground improvements and repairs to the floodlights plus players' wages were the main causes. In an interview after the meeting the Chairman Mr P Culley said "Changes are unavoidable if we were to stay in the League and try to advance from last season's crises." He went on to say "It is not a large amount when you take into consideration what has been done by the Club."

It was also reported that the wages structure for the new season would be trimmed severely. The meeting saw a proposal to increase membership fees but the proposal was not carried. The standard election of officers following the AGM saw the confirmation of Television comedy star Jack Smethurst as President, Peter Culley was re-elected as Chairman with Les Mangan as Vice-Chairman, John Olney Treasurer, Nick Vince General Secretary, and Wally Doman as

Chesham United 1983-1984

71

Chesham United 1983-1984

Tony Currie

fixtures secretary. The rest of the committee was John West, Bob Batchelor, Tony Lowton and Bob Day.

Tony Currie made 12 appearances for Chesham in the season. This season started on 20 August and created a lot of interest with TV and the media. He played for the Club because of his brother Paul who had recently returned from Canada. His first competitive game was against Hornchurch at Tring Town's Pendley ground. Over 700 people turned out and Chesham won 3-0, G Cordice, B Greenhaugh and R Tavinor the scorers. His final game on 31 March 1984 was against Aveley at Hemel Hempstead, Chesham winning 2-0 with Tony and Micky Gilchrist scoring.

On 23 August the Club had another set back when the Club Chairman and main sponsor resigned. This happened at Slough, with a game against Boreham Wood FC. The problem started with the team refusing to wear "gold line" logo shirts designed for the winter. Mr Culley had been unhappy about the way the Club was going for some time and this incident was the last straw, especially as the time he spent working for the Club was affecting his business.

1984-85 season
On 4 December Graham Taylor, the Manager of Watford Football Club brought a full strength first team to play for the opening of the new stand. It was an attractive game with Watford winning 3-1. Matt Strange was the Chesham scorer. The Chesham team were Baguley, Lewis, Currie, Morrissey, M Martin, Thompson, O'Driscoll, Lay, Ryan, Franks, C Martin, Strange and Bennett.

Chesham United v Watford 4 December 1984
The first match played after the opening of the new stand

Les Mangan took over as Chairman of the Club but struggled to steady the ship. A loan was obtained from a local bank with a number of Club supporters acting as guarantors, in desperate hope of saving the ailing Club. In February Mr Mangan resigned due to the stress of the position and had a heart attack. Due to the lack of money and high wages the Club Manager was sacked. Pat Morrissey had seen Chesham through the most testing period in its history.

His position was taken on a temporary basis by George Martin, the father of Mick and Chris who were current players. Mr B Lay and Mr D Hopkins were his back up men.

With all the problems surrounding the Club some really good results on the field were achieved. A 1-0 win over Aylesbury FC early on resulted in the Club reaching the final of the Senior County Cup. The final took place at Maidenhead's ground on 13 April against Wokingham Town FC. Chesham's team were Baguley, Corteen, Lewis, Thompson, M Martin, Casemore, Strange, Lay, Ryan, Franks, and C Martin with substitutes Jacks and Bates. Chesham were under strength because of the loss of some of the first team players through the previous sackings. Although Wokingham had a strong team, United only lost by only a single goal. The final itself was something of a highlight for most of the Chesham supporters in what was a very uneasy season. The match report read as follows:

"The 1984-1985 Berks and Bucks Senior Cup Final
Saturday April 13th 1985 played at Maidenhead United
Chesham United 0 - Wokingham Town 1

Following their excellent 1-0 victory over local rivals Aylesbury United in the semi-final, Chesham were paired with Isthmian Premier top six side Wokingham Town in this year's final. The fixture was traditionally played on Easter Monday, but has now been switched to a Saturday. This year's Final took place at York Road, home of Maidenhead United FC.

Chesham took about 250 supporters to the match, who helped swell the crowd to 700. Unusually, it was the less fancied side from Division one who had the most support on the day. The match was played, however in dreadful conditions. Intermittent showers ensured that the playing surface was slippery, but the decisive factor was the gale force wind blowing lengthways down the pitch. It made controlled football and precision passing out of the question and while the goalkeeper at one end struggled to get the ball up to the half way line, the goalkeeper at the other end often watched his kicks sail over the players in the middle and land in the arms of his opposite number.

Martin Baguley, the Club's longest-serving player

Chesham won the toss and decided to play against the wind, but towards the covered end at York Road, where the majority of Chesham supporters were massed in their distinctive claret and blue colours. Both sides started hesitantly, trying to come to terms with the wind which tended to put off the more skilful players. However, after only three minutes, Laurie Ryan was put clean through a rather square defence. He ran on but saw his shot well pushed away by Wokingham keeper Frank Parsons. Both sides struggled to gain control of midfield, but trying to push the ball wide and attack down the flanks often only saw the ball swing away in the wind and into touch. Chances were few and far between, although John Franks did try a long shot that dipped late, but was always going over the bar. At the other end, a McMahon shot from twenty yards looked goal bound, but was brilliantly tipped over the bar by Martin Baguley at full stretch. Then, in the 31st minute came the deciding goal - a goal fit to be the winner in any cup final, no matter what level. Wokingham's young blond striker Richard Evans created some space for himself some 25 yards out. Without hesitating , he looked up and then hit a pile driver past the despairing dive of Martin Baguley. Baguley, who had often saved Chesham this season, was given absolutely no chance. United tried to press forward before half time but were met with both the wind and some resolute defence by Wokingham, in which coloured full-back Kirk Corbin was particularly impressive.

On several occasions, the Wokingham keeper (and former Football League player), Frank Parsons broke the new law forbidding goalkeepers to roll the ball along the ground, pick it up again and then clear it. Despite howls of protest from the Chesham supporters behind the goal the referee chose to repeatedly ignore this. Although, at the other end, Wokingham tried to expose Chesham in the air, Martin Baguley in goal and the centre-back pairing of Tony Thompson and Mick Martin held firm. Wokingham's highly talented midfield player Neal Stanley, tried to create openings on United's right flank and managed to force a couple of corners but was not up to his usual penetrative best. After 61 minutes, Wokingham's Dave Cox had to be substituted after a clash of heads in one of Chesham's raids. With the result beginning to appear settled, Chesham's caretaker Manager, George Martin, tried a different combination by taking off Laurie Ryan and pushing young Raymond Jack into the fray. A couple of minutes later, Paul Bates came on for Chris Martin. In the last ten minutes, both sides had chances. A Paul Bates' shot went over the bar while for Wokingham, a lightening raid saw a bad miss by Evans with the goal at his mercy. For Chesham, a Barry Casemore free-kick just flashed past the post, but the more Chesham attacked, the more they were exposed at the back.

In the end, Wokingham ran out worthy and comfortable winners to the delight of their fans. Not a classic, the wind saw to that, but a fine achievement by Chesham to reach the final and put a good show for their loyal fans."

1985-86 season
From May 1985 to the end of the year the future of Chesham United was in the balance. It was on 31 May that a local businessman Mr Howard Lambert took over as the Chairman. His intention was to form a limited company and he spent many hours trying to get to the bottom of the financial problems surrounding the Club.

After many weeks he found that the actual amount owed was in the region of £95,000 after which he stated "Now is the time to show courage and character". For a short period in July 1985 Nick Vince took over as caretaker team boss, this a month that turned sour for many United supporters. After receiving no money for the loan for some time, the Bank decided to call in all the guarantees. The amount of money called in was about £23,000, a drop in the ocean when it was realised that the Club owed over £100,000 because of the high interest rates of the time.

The guarantors were mostly made up of true Chesham United supporters who really did play their part in keeping the Club going. Indeed it would be true to say that without these people the Club would have folded there and then. Press comments such as " Chesham United FC will die in 13 days", highlighted the situation to the public. In order to raise the funds all 92 clubs in the Football League received a letter asking if they could contribute or donate memorabilia for raffles or auctions. A football pools scheme called "Top Score" was launched.

On 12 July Howard Lambert along with Brian Greenhalgh resigned. A quote from Mr Greenhalgh stated " I could not see any future in taking over a Club with no apparent stability". 6 August saw Chesham take on Swindon Town in a friendly at the Meadow. The match was arranged to help the Club raise funds. The Swindon Town manager at that time was Mr Lou Macari, who brought a very useful squad down to the Club. Chesham had on show their new manager Dave Russell, along with chief coach Alan Ackrel. Richard Tavinor was the third member of the team and he took part in the coaching and training. The game against Swindon ended in a 2-0 win for the visitors. As the season approached changes were taking place in league sponsorship. The Isthmian league was to be known as the Vauxhall-Opel League, with the new sponsors injected cash into advertising around the grounds in the form of flags and banners.

How Chesham managed to start the season with all the financial crisis that surrounded them is still a mystery. On 9 August a four strong group of businessmen which included ex-Chairman Mr Howard Lambert, formed a company called Smallwood Enterprises Ltd, its aim being to try and save Chesham United. Chesham started the season with an FA Cup defeat away to Barton Rovers and then went on to beat Boreham Wood in the league. Finchley knocked United out of the trophy after a replay. As cup runs are good money spinners this was not a very good start, the league position after 11 games saw the club fourth from bottom.

By 20 August Smallwood Enterprises were considering pulling out of the deal to try and save the Club. Apparently the men concerned did not realise or know that the brewers Wethereds Ltd had a charge on the lease. Also in August tucked away in one corner of the local sports paper was the headline "Mr A Aplin resigns from Chilterns Rugby Club" a move that was to have a very big bearing on Chesham's future.

In November Chesham had moved up the league a few places from the bottom, Wembley were top having lost only one game in fourteen. From August to November the Club had numerous general meetings to try and solve the financial problems. By the end of November after the last meeting Nick Vince decided to fight on for the Club. It was around this time that Smallwood Enterprises pulled out altogether from their rescue bid.

In the early part of 1985 other negotiations were taking place between Club officials and a local builder and developer, with plans being made to improve the Club's other sports facilities. Because of the lack of meetings, communication with committee members was not very good and as a result a few members resigned. Minutes were lost and it seemed that the general public knew more about the Club than the committee. The saga with the local builders went on for some time and in February 1985 they wrote to the Club stating that "Any development could be a long and tortuous process which could only be negotiated if the football club could maintain a unified steady and consistent position."

In April that lease was transferred to the local builders, but they had to pay for the charge on the lease.

On the football side Chesham were struggling to stay in the league. In January Wembley came to the Meadow for a league game, at this point they were top with 47 points from 23 games. Chesham remained in 10th place, one point above Leytonstone and Ilford. The result was a 2-2 draw and a well earned point for Chesham. It is a sad reflection that when United played them again in April Wembley were still top of the league and Chesham were doomed for the drop. Out of the remaining 18 games played during this period, United won 3, lost 12, and drew 3. Nothing could save the Club from starting the following season in division 2. Movements to save the Club continued during the closed season.

1986-87 season
During the 1986-87 season Chesham United embarked upon their biggest struggle to survive. At the close of the 1986 season local businessmen were trying to solve Chesham's financial problems and to give the Club some future. On one side was a consortium headed by Mr B Wells, and on the other was a local builder, who was the lease holder.

On Monday 2 June 1986 the local builder took possession of Chesham United FC as the lease holder. Straight away Mr Wells and his consortium sprung into action and he outlined his plans to the committee members of the Club. Chesham United would become a Limited company headed by a Board of Directors. On Thursday 26 June an extraordinary general meeting was held to discuss the situation with the members. The Directors designate would be six; Mr B Wells, Mr J Conrad, Mr J Burton, Mr R Old, Mr S McDonnell, and Mr A Aplin.

With all the uncertainty that was surrounding the Club, Dave Russell the manager was not sure about his future. There was a EGM to be held on 26 June and Russell was hoping to start pre-season training on 8 July, which did not seem to leave much time to get the players required. It seemed that Russell was in no man's land. On 19 June Tony Aplin was confirmed as Chairman designate of the proposed Chesham United FC Ltd board of directors. The meeting of the 26th was held in the clubhouse, but it was uncertain whether the meeting had been properly convened. After some long discussions another meeting was planned for 8 July.

On 27 June it was announced that Nick Vince was to resign as Club Secretary. He had worked hard for the Club over many years and he kept it going during its most difficult times. Most people found him hard to work with but during the last few months in his role as Club secretary he carried out most of the Club's duties on his own. These would be taken over for the time being by Mr W Doman.

Chesham United 1986-1987

On Thursday 8 July 1986 another EGM was held for the members of Chesham to decide whether to form a limited company to be known as Chesham United FC Ltd. It was recorded as one of the fastest meetings in the Club's history, four minutes and thirty seconds. Following the meeting a new management committee was formed headed by Mr A Warboys, the rest of the committee consisted of Mr S McDonnell, Mr W Doman, Mr J Pearce, Mr R Charlton, and Mr J Burton, who would be liaison officer between both the management committee and the social committee. A few people opposed the idea but generally most knew that it was the only way forward for the Club to survive, so it looked as if Chesham United could and would have a future.

Chesham United's new supporters' and social committee was made up of the following: Chairman Mr R Charlton, Vice-Chairman Mr J Pearce, Mr K Hancock Secretary, Mr R Day Treasurer, Mr T Greenham, Mr R Aris, Mr F Price, Mr S Holt, Mr J Martin, Mrs I MacDonnell, Mrs E Morgan, and Mr H Doman. These supporters helped to carry out match day duties and arrange social events.

Before that start of the season Chesham had new sponsor W Old the Civil Engineering and Building Firm. But yet another blow was to hit the Club, the manager Dave Russell decided to give up for personal reasons, but he stayed on at the Club as a player. The job was taken over by Jim Hegarty as caretaker-manager. Jim put a lot of faith in his youth players and in the end this was his downfall. In the first league match of the new season Chesham were at home to Rainham Town. The result was a 1-0 win, the goal coming from Godfrey Cordice. On the following Tuesday Chesham won 2-0 away at Ware. Bennett and Jones scored the goals, and it seemed that Chesham had got the start they wanted.

In the AC Delco Cup Chesham beat Egham Town 2-0. There were five changes to the team that started the season and as regards team performance this was not very impressive. The first league defeat came against Wivenhoe Town away with a score of 5-2. In the FA Cup Preliminary round Chesham were drawn at home to the Met Police. The Club and supporters expected a good Cup run, but this match held many surprises. By half time Chesham were losing 1-0, but with still all to play for in the second half, Chesham came out with lots of enthusiasm but just after the start they seemed to have a complete black-out. Met Police scored another seven goals

Another piece of silverware for the trophy cabinet

in reply to Chesham's one, the final result being 8-1. This turned out to be one of the Club's biggest defeats for some time and as Jim Hegarty came out of the dug out he could see Chesham's new manager sitting in the stand and he knew his time was up.

By 8 September Barry Gould had been appointed the new manager of United. Jim Hegarty's time as caretaker-manager had only lasted 17 days, but in that time he ran both the first and second teams. This meant double the pressure and double the work load.

Barry Gould's first game was in the league against Letchworth, the result was a 1-1 draw, M Martin scoring Chesham's goal. The first home game was against Clapton, 88 supporters turned up and this was one of the lowest gates of the season. The result was a 3-0 win for the home side. By 27 September Chesham had gone to the top of the league, a complete turn round for the Club. When September had come and gone Mr Gould was named as manager of the month for division two of the Vauxhall-Opel league north. Wins against Erith, Belvedere, Royston, Cheshunt and Hemel Hempstead all helped to bring Mr Gould his reward. Some new players had been bought by the club, Francis Araquez, a very talented attacking defender, was one of the players to add flair to Chesham's game. On 26 December Chesham were still top and looking like a team that could win the Division two Championship. By 1 January the Club was 8 points clear and two games in hand. When Chesham played Tring Town on 8 February a few points had been lost, through defeats by Wolverton 2-0, and Clapton 3-1, and draws against Heybridge Swifts and Hertford slowed the club down in its quest for the championship.

In April Chesham headed the league from Wolverton Town, nine points clear. The crunch game for this month was against Harringay Borough, who were lying third in the league. At the end of April Chesham had done the double over Harringay this time winning 3-2, the result ensuring the Club would play first division football next season. When Chesham played Letchworth Garden City on 29 April and won 1-0 the championship was in the bag. The goal came from Araquez. In April Mr B Gould had won his second manager of the month award. All the hard work from the players and volunteers had paid off. Chesham United were in Division one for the start of the 1987-88 season and the survival of the Club was secure.

1987-88 season
The 1987/88 season was the Centenary of the Club's recognition by the FA and the Club had some very attractive games lined up. One hundred years of football and yet last year who would have thought the Club would still be in existence. Both the FA and the Berks & Bucks FA presented the Club with illuminated addresses to commemorate the occasion. Before the start of the season many changes took place around the ground and at management level. During the close season volunteer workers from the supporters and social and management committees rolled up their sleeves and got to work improving the ground. A concrete pathway around the outside of the pitch was laid, complete fencing around the ground with gates and entrances, improved dug outs, a new family enclosure and improved hard standing for spectators. The work was directly attributable to the personal financial support given by the Directors of Chesham United FC Ltd. The clubhouse was totally refurbished, again financed by the directors. The Club sponsor for the season was William Old. The biggest shock to hit the supporters and general public was the dismissal of the manager, Barry Gould.

The man who took his place was John Delaney, the ex-Wycombe Wanderer player and non-league international. His assistant was Tony Horsfall. Unlike Barry Gould, John Delaney had a very good pedigree in non-league football and the Chesham board hoped that his knowledge would help Chesham achieve its ambition of premier football.

A few friendly matches had been arranged before the start of the league programme, these

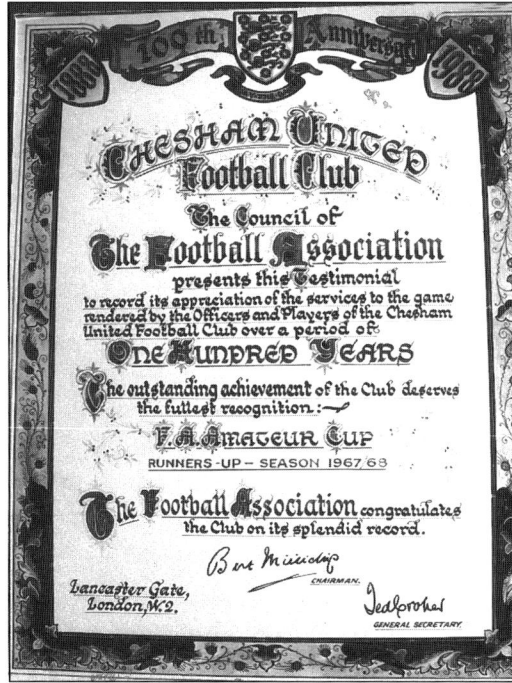

Illuminated Scroll commemorating Chesham's 100 years in Senior Football

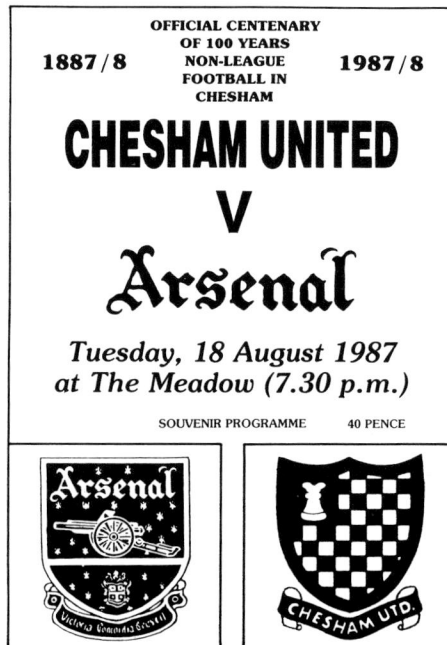

Souvenir Programme for the game against Arsenal

were against Bedfont Athletic, Harefield United, and Chertsey. It was unfortunate that one of the players to depart was G Cordice who joined D Russell at Marlow FC. Cordice was a big centre forward who scored many goals.

Everyone at the Meadow was looking forward to seeing Arsenal FC on 18 August. As promised a very good Arsenal squad turned up and the team that played was: Willmott, Francis, Winterburn, Ball, Stolley, Morrow, Caesar, Quinn, Groves, Rix with substitutes Hillier and Connolly. The Chesham squad were: Baguley, Butfoy, Dockery, St Hilaire, Martin, Hoare, Perna, Watt, Davies, McGuinness, Richardson. Substitutes were Conroy, Smethurst, Jeffrey, Holt, and Gilchrist. The result was a 3-1 win for Arsenal scored by Groves and Connelly with an own goal from St Hilaire. Chesham's goal was scored by Mick Martin, who also had a very good game. 1,600 fans turned up to watch a very entertaining game of football.

League action started on 22 August with the first game at home to Walton and Hersham. The result was a 1-1 draw. Both teams playing tight football and gave very little away. In the AC Delco Cup a 4-3 home win was recorded against Tilbury FC, which gave Chesham a home draw against Worthing FC. Again the home Club turned it on to win 5-1. In the following round Chesham played Yeovil Town and lost 3-0. In the FA Cup an away draw meant going up to Gorleston where one goal separated the teams with Gorleston winning. On 3 October Banbury United entertained Chesham in the FA Trophy. Although the home side went 1-0 down early on Chesham just crumbled and lost the game 3-1. Many travelling fans slow hand-clapped the team off the pitch after this game.

During this time many football league clubs were watching Martin St Hilaire, who was known as the jewel in Chesham's team. Barnsley, Wolves and Brighton being just a few. By the beginning of October Chesham were seventh in the league with some fine results against such teams as Leatherhead 2-1, Basildon 2-0 and Walthamstow Avenue 2-1. It was a very weak United side that played Woking FC in the league on 20 October and lost 2-0. Also during October Delaney released his assistant, Tony Horsfall. His successor was Dave Holt, who had played for Chesham in midfield in the 1980s.

On 14 November Marlow played Chesham in the league at the Meadow, with the Marlow team containing a number of ex-Chesham players. Managed by Dave Russell, Araquez and Cordice lined up against their old team. The result was a 2-2 draw, which kept Marlow second in the league with Grays Athletic top.

The reign of the manager Mr Delaney came to an end in December. In a statement he said "I'm not enjoying it anymore". It was a very difficult job for him to do when you consider that he had to step into the shoes of a manager that had won the league championship. On 12 December the Club announced that John Pratt, the former Tottenham Hotspur player, would be taking over as caretaker manager. John Pratt had a very difficult job, the morale of the players was very low and the Club's spirits needed lifting. He did not have any experience at this level and it took some time before the players understood his methods but by the end of the season you could see his experience as a professional coming across.

In January it was confirmed that Mr Pratt had accepted the job as Chesham's manager properly. In the early part of February Tony Thompson re-joined the club after a short spell with Dunstable. Tony was one of the players that left the Club after the team was reshuffled by the former manager.

Chesham had to wait until 13 February for the first win under the guidance of John Pratt. This came against Staines Town in the league away. The result was 3-2 on what could only be described as a mud heap of a pitch. Harding, Watt, and Thompson scored the goals to secure the points. When Woking FC played Chesham again in the league on 20 February every point was important. Woking were lying third from the top and Chesham were third from the bottom.

The game ended in a 1-1 draw with Woking being awarded a penalty in the fifth minute of injury time. Alan Paradis scored Chesham's goal in the 15th minute. Chesham made up for this the following week by putting 5 goals past Hampton FC in the league, with goals by Watt, Conroy (twice), Hilaire and Barber.

During the next few weeks Chesham produced some good results. A win against Southwick FC 2-0 and draws against Oxford 1-1, Walthamstow 0-0 and Lewes 2-2, kept the Club's hopes alive. It was on the 9 April that another 5-0 win was recorded. This time it was at home to Wolverton. Watt and Conroy scored twice each and Hilaire once. Two defeats followed this, Wembley 2-1 and Kingsbury 0-4, which put Chesham very close to the relegation zone.

On 19 April Northampton Town played at the Meadow in the second game to celebrate the centenary. The game took place on a rain soaked evening, a very poor crowd of 80 turned up for this one and the match ended in a 3-3 draw.

In the league the pressure was building on the players, with concern as to whether the Club could avoid the drop back into Division two after just one season in Division one. The last two games in the league saw journeys to the coast, the first against another club struggling at the bottom, Worthing. In this match Chesham took the lead after 13 minutes with a goal from Steve Conroy but the home team equalised after 41 minutes when Tony Thompson gave away a penalty. This made the half time score 1-1. In the second half both teams played tight football and the final score was 1-1. This meant that in the last game of the season at Southwick on the Bank Holiday Monday Chesham had to win.

Chesham arrived at Southwick with a very hard job to do. The game turned out to be very entertaining considering the amount of pressure on the players. The score at half time was 0-1 to Chesham, Richardson got the first in 44 minutes. In the second half Chesham continued to put pressure on the home club and for long spells dominated the game. Early in the second half Chesham increased their lead with a goal from Johnny Barber after 62 minutes to 0-2. Southwick got back into the game soon after this to make the score 1-2. Chesham's survival was assured in the 90th minute when again Johnny Barber took the ball away on the half way line and ran straight for the goal, leaving the Southwick defence in a complete mess. He rounded the home goalkeeper to score the most important goal of the season to make the final score 1-3.

1988-89 season

Before the start of the season the Club in association with Catlins Limited, the car dealers in Chesham, set up a sponsorship deal worth in the region of £30,000 over three years. The deal at the time was one of the best sponsorships in non league football. The sponsorship was set up by Chesham's commercial manager at the time Brian Richardson in conjunction with Robert Catlin of Catlins Limited. The Chesham squad was made up with some talented players, Watt, Benning, Conroy, Lowe to name just a few. Local players such as Richardson, Wells, Baguley, and Martin were also included in the line-up.

One of Chesham's warm up games was against a Tottenham Hotspur XI. The team consisted of youth and reserves with the inspiration of then talented Chris Hugton at full back. The game itself turned out to be a bit of a flop as regards entertainment with Spurs winning 0-2. Another friendly was played against Marlow, this game was played on a Tuesday evening at Marlow. The result of this game was another defeat for Chesham 2-1, Davies and Stone scored for Marlow with a Conroy goal for Chesham.

Chesham's league campaign started with an away game against Walton and Hersham on 20 August. In a very even game the score at half time was 0-0. In the second half Chesham were awarded a free kick. Watt took the kick which was deflected off a defender into the goal to give

Chesham United 1987-1988

Chesham the lead 1-0, from this point the home team put Chesham under a lot of pressure, but with some fine work from Baguley in goal Chesham held on to the points. Seven days later Chesham played their first home game against Wivenhoe Town. The game was a blow for Chesham as they lost to a Paul Harrison goal in the second half.

On 30 August Chesham lost their second league game, this time to Boreham Wood 1-2. Not a very good start to the season from a team expected to do well. When Chesham played Hornchurch FC in the FA Cup preliminary round on 3 September they had played three league games with one win and two defeats. Hornchurch proved to be no push over in this game. Man of the match for Chesham was St Hilaire who tormented the Hornchurch defence all afternoon, but in the end Chesham could only manage a draw 1-1, Martin equalising after 36 minutes. Hornchurch had taken the lead on the 25th minute from a Stuart Jukes goal. The replay was a eleven goal thriller played during midweek at Bridge Avenue, Hornchurch. The score after 90 minutes was 4-4, after Chesham had trailed 1-2 at half time. During extra time Chesham ran out winners thanks to a John Watt penalty after 103 minutes. The final score was a 5-6 win for Chesham. In the next round Chesham were drawn away to Hayes, a game that Hayes won 0-1. In the other Cups Basingstoke knocked Chesham out of the FA Trophy 1-3 after Chesham had beaten Collier Row in the previous round. In the A C Delco Cup (League Cup) Chesham beat Bognor Regis 4-1 at home, and then lost in a replay at home to Croydon after extra time. Wycombe Wanderers put Chesham out of the Berks and Bucks Senior Cup 1-4.

The Club's main concern now was to improve on its league position. On 10 September Basingstoke gave a lesson on how to score goals by inflicting a 7-0 defeat on the Club in the league. Defeat also followed at the hands of Uxbridge 1-3. When Chesham played the Met Police on 8 October 1988 a new manager was leading the team out. Pat Morrissey had returned. This was Pat's second spell as manager of Chesham. His right hand man was going to be Alan Randall. Most of Alan's career had been spent at Hendon FC. Because of John Pratt and his assistant Dave Holt's lack of success with only seven wins from twenty nine league games and the thought of relegation looming the Directors felt this was the best move for the Club. It took Pat and Alan some time to put Chesham back on its feet.

The much respected Alan Moore sadly passed away on 26 February. Alan was 65 and was Chesham's Chairman when the club played at Wembley in the 1968 Amateur Cup final.

By April Chesham's position in the league had improved. A 3-1 away win over Collier Row had secured Chesham's future in division one for another season. Chesham United supporters' player of the year was Neil Bartlett. Before the season came to an end it was apparent that the Directors were not happy with the way the team had performed. It was in early May that Pat Morrissey was asked to step down as manager. The new manager would be the former West Ham and Bournemouth AFC player Alan Taylor. Other changes were taking place within the Club. Mr Syd MacDonnell was standing down as Club Secretary and Treasurer, his place was to be taken by Mr Bill McGowen. Bobby Peck would be Alan Taylor's assistant manager.

1989-90 season

When Alan Taylor took over not many supporters could name all the managers since 1983, most ran out of fingers. Tony Aplin the Club's Chairman was determined to get the right man. Alan Taylor was in probably the hottest seat in non-league football. Alan spent many weeks in search of good players, scouting at many clubs. Apart from Graves, Dave Sansom the ex-Barnet star signed for the Club. Paddy McCarthy and Jeff Willis who both played for G M Conference club Farnborough also joined Chesham. Retained players included Steve Wallace, Steve Cordery, Martin St Hilaire, Neil Bartlett, Tony Thompson and Peter Brown. The biggest signing was Dave Sansom who cost the Club in the region of £10,000, a large amount for a non-league club. Stuart Atkins also returned to Chesham.

Off the field the clubhouse was being totally refurbished. A total sum of £180,000 was spent, including work on the grandstand, the popular stand, pitch and other groundworks. In July the squad was back in training for the start of next season.

One of the season's attractions at the Meadow was a friendly against Fulham FC. Fulham won the game 0-2. Another friendly against Basingstoke had also been arranged, Basingstoke won this game 0-5. Many changes took place within Chesham team on both occasions.

When Chesham played St Albans in the last game before the start of the season the team Alan Taylor put out seemed to have got it right with a 2-1 win. Chesham's league action started with a home game against Southwick FC. Chesham had an impressive 2-0 win with goals from Cordery and Sansom.

The first away game was against Uxbridge FC and this proved to be another good performance with Chesham recording a 1-2 win. Britnell and Sansom's penalty were the goals. After this good start the rot started to set in again with defeats by Boreham Wood 0-2, Woking 2-4, Dorking 1-2, and Wivenhoe 0-1, in the league and after a draw away to Aveley in the FA Cup, a 1-2 lost replay. Burnham knocked Chesham out of the Trophy 0-1.

One bright light was a 4-1 win at home over Egham Town in the AC Delco Cup. With the money available to spend on top class players, Alan Taylor stuck to his plan of building up the squad he had over a period of time, and this proved to be his downfall. On 18 September 1989 the board parted company with him. The next manager was John Clements. John certainly injected new life into the Club and it is true to say the players that he and assistant Keith Collins brought into the team brought about United's tuning point.

John Clements came from Windsor and Eton FC where he spent three years as the Royals' manager. His football career was spent at Reading AFC followed by periods as a player and manager with Slough, Marlow, Dunstable and Burnham. John's first game in charge of Chesham was a 0-1 defeat, but the main thing was that the team showed a lot of determination something that had been lacking in the past. When Chesham played Hampton away in the league there were nine changes to the team. One of the most significant signings was that of Andy Lomas from Barnet AFC, a move that cost in the regions of £25,000. Other signings included Paul Benning from Wycombe, Brian Cooper from Slough, Dermot Drummy from Hendon and

Keith Baker from Farnborough. All played in the Hampton game, the new look Chesham put up a fine performance to run out 1-2 winners with the goals from Wallace.

During the next few months Darren Angell, Sean Norman, Mark Dawber, and Steve Bateman joined the Club along with £15,000 Frances Cassidy from Harrow Borough. Chesham's position in the league improved and a good 1-2 win in the Berks & Bucks Senior Cup against Marlow generated more enthusiasm. Paul Benning and Steve Hetze scored the goals. Steve Hetze joined Chesham from Reading AFC and later took on the coaching role at Chesham.

At the beginning of January it was announced that John Clements had won the Manager of the month for December. It was in December that Chesham signed an American by the name of Eric Maki. Unfortunately he never played a competitive game for the Club because of injury. Chesham's hopes for promotion went when in February a very good Woking team beat them 1-0. In the Berks & Bucks Senior Cup Chesham reached the semi-finals with a home draw against Wycombe Wanderers. The result was a 0-2 win for Wycombe, but Chesham put up a very brave fight after playing most of the game without goalkeeper Andy Lomas, who was lost through injury.

In the quarter final of the AC Delco Cup Chesham were at home to St Albans. The home club went 0-2 down at half time but in the second half Price got a goal back in the 85th minute. Chesham put pressure on St Albans goal but the final score was a 1-2 win to St Albans. In March Dave Sansom was transfer listed for a week. During the week John Clements stated that differences had been resolved and Dave Sansom was taken off the transfer list. When March arrived Chesham were in negotiations for two top class players Micky Barnes and Michael Banton. Both players went from Windsor and Eton to Barnet AFC while Chesham were trying to sign them but in the end Chesham got their men. Both players were instrumental in Chesham's success over the next few seasons. The fee for these players was reputed to be in region of £50,000. Players that left the Club in a major shake up were Steve Hezte, Neil Bartlett and later Glen Price. Strikers Mark Butler and Mark Dawber who were on the transfer list were later taken off. It was Mark Butler, Mick Barnes and Keith Baker who were selected to play for the Vauxhall League against Slough, Mark Butler scoring the first goal in a 1-4 win for the league side.

John Clements was trying out a new formation with which Chesham had a small amount of success. The formation was 5-2-1-2 and at one point during the early part of the season Chesham made third place using this style of play. After a short spell this new style was dropped and Club reverted back to a more conventional style. As the season came to an end Chesham had a goal famine that lasted over four games without scoring a goal. This came to an end with a 4-1 home win against Lewes FC. The Club's player of the year was goalkeeper Andy Lomas.

1990-91 season

Just before that start of the season Chesham made several signings. Among them were Byron Walton, a hardworking centre forward and Gary Attrell a very fast midfield attacking player. Gary turned out to be one of the most exciting players ever to put on a Chesham shirt. Other players joining were Steve Emmanuel and Mick O'Shea. One player to leave was Mark Butler.

The reserves were disbanded but an Under 18 squad was formed and managed by Nigel Franklin who at the time was commercial manager. The U18's played in the Allied Counties Midweek Youth league. The Club's friendlies before the start of the season were against Brentford AFC with a very creditable 1-1 draw for Chesham. Marlow came to the Meadow next and this also resulted in a 1-1 draw. In this game the home Club showed that they were just as good as their premier league neighbours. Chertsey FC felt the pressure of Chesham's forwards in the next friendly losing 4-2. In a friendly played at Newlands Park Chesham beat Maidenhead United 4-0. The most impressive of all the pre-season games was the one away to Weymouth.

Chesham sunk the seasiders 0-3. Goals from Lindo, Banton and Cassidy put Chesham in a good frame of mind for the start of the season that saw Chesham as favourites for the league title.

Off the field the Club held its AGM and formed a new management structure consisting of the following officers, Chairman L Gwilliam, W McGowan, A Greenham, L King, G Bartlett, E Bartlett, M Howe, R Day, K Hancock, R Glenister, F Price, C Dunkerton and B Monagle. It all seemed set for a very interesting and exciting season. The league action started with an away game at Southwick FC.

The first home game for the senior team was against Tooting and Mitcham FC. The game itself turned out to be a very drab 0-0 draw and there was still no sign of the form that Chesham had shown in the pre-season matches. It took Chesham three league games to show their true form. The unfortunate team to suffer was Whyteleafe FC at the Meadow. The result was a 7-2 thumping with Banton and Walton each bagging a hat trick. Lindo scored the other goal. This win was followed with a 0-3 away win at Uxbridge. In the FA Cup Baldock Town came to the Meadow and were defeated 4-1, Banton, Williams (another new signing) and Lindo bagging the goals. Two surprising defeats followed, away to Chalfont St Peter 0-1, and 2-0 at home to Molesey FC. Another new signing appeared, D Payne, although it turned out later that he was on loan from Barnet FC.

After six games in the league Chesham held a mid table position with Hitchin Town on top. Back in the FA Cup after a draw at home to Hertford Town the replay resulted in a 1-5 win for Chesham. The FA Trophy produced a big shock for St Albans City who lost 4-0 at the Meadow. In the same month, September, Enfield FC knocked Chesham out of the FA Cup 0-3 also at the Meadow. This was a very hard game for the home Club, particularly as M Barnes was sent off for allegedly punching Enfield's Paul Furlong. After this game another knock out was landed on manager John Clements. John lasted just one season. Dave Brown took over as caretaker manager, and during his time the Club had four wins and two defeats from six games.

Hendon FC won the first round replay of the FA cup 1-2 at the Meadow after Chesham held them to a 1-1 draw at Hendon, Bateman scoring with a late penalty. Chesham had more luck in the Trophy with a good 1-2 away win at Tamworth. Goal scorers for Chesham were Thompson and Walton. This was Tamworth's first defeat of the season and Lomas had a particularly

Chesham United 1990-1991

outstanding game in goal. During the week up to 3 November the Club announced the appointment of the new manager, George Borg.

George Borg's background in football is impressive. Signed by West Ham as a schoolboy he later moved to Millwall AFC and played for the first team at the age of 16. He played for some years in South Africa before returning to England and then played for Brenford AFC. Later he decided to play non-league football and so joined Dulwich Hamlet FC before moving to Wycombe Wanderers for £2,000, a record for Wycombe at the time. After four years he moved on again this time to Dartford FC and played in the team that won the championship.

Later he joined Maidstone under Barry Fry. His first manager's job was at Barking FC where he saved them from relegation before moving to Chelmsford. Dave Brown took on the role as assistant manager. George's first game in charge was on 3 November away to Croydon FC. Chesham won this game 0-4 and went on to a record 15 games without defeat. This form put the Club on top of the league by 11 December. A player called Billy Goldstone joined the Club with George. Billy scored many fine goals during his stay at the Club and was a very important member of the team.

In the Trophy Chesham had another impressive win this time away to Marlow FC 1-2, Walton and Thompson again scoring the goals. Enfield FC felt the force of Chesham on 12 December when revenge was sweet in the Loctite Cup. Chesham won 2-1 at the Meadow. Cosby scored both the goals. Unfortunately the Enfield jinx was again in operation on 12 January when in injury time they knocked Chesham out of the Trophy first round proper. Paul Furlong got the goal in what was a very fine performance by the away team. About this time Mark Jones took over as Commercial Manager and Mrs McMonagle also joined the management staff. In January George Borg was named manager of the month. Also Chesham were awarded an "A" grade from the Vauxhall League for the ground. This enabled the Club to progress if or when they were to win promotion to the premier league. Chesham still managed to do well in the league and by 12 March they were top of the league with Bromley FC in second place. In the Loctite Cup an away game at Lewes FC produced a 0-1 win for Chesham. George himself played.

Both Burnham FC and Abingdon United FC were defeated away, 2-3 and 0-3 respectively, in the Berks & Bucks Senior Cup before Chesham reached the semi-final against Wycombe Wanderers, which was played at the new Adams Park ground. Chesham produced some excellent football and a score of 3-1 to the home club flattered them not a little. Gary Attrell scored Chesham's goal.

Chesham showed again that they can compete with the best. Chesham's team was: Lomas, Goldstone, Norman, May, Barnes, Benning, Dawber, Engwell, Cosby, Walton, and Attrell, with substitutes Banton and Thompson. On 23 March Bromley came to the Meadow in a top of the table league match, billed as the battle of the giants. Bromley still felt that they could over take Chesham and win the championship. This game turned out to be a typical top of the league clash, and Bromley spoilt the game somewhat with their tactics of time wasting. Chesham gave Bromley all three points with a bad mistake in defence allowing the away club a 0-1 win. The game degenerated at times and when Warren May was sent off this did not help the home Club's cause.

Another new player Wayne Turner who made his debut against Dulwich Hamlet had a good game. The quarter finals of the Loctite Cup produced a home game against Dagenham FC, another club from the premier league. Chesham pulled out all the stops for this game and put on a superb display of football. On an evening when the home Club were looking for goals by half time they were 3-0 up. The final score was 5-1, with two goals from Banton, and one each for Bateman, Cosby and Turner. The win in this game gave Chesham a two leg semi-final against local rivals Aylesbury also from the premier league. The game was to take place in April.

Southwick FC came to the Meadow on 3 April in the return league match. Chesham had lost to Southwick in the first league game of the season so the home Club were looking for revenge. It came in the form of a 8-0 defeat for the visitors. Chesham again produced the goals with Banton scoring four, Bateman one, Cosby two and Dawber one.

The first leg of the Loctite Cup was played on 18 April at Aylesbury's ground in torrential rain. Aylesbury were favourites to win this game having themselves had a good season in the premier league. Again Chesham raised their game and after 15 minutes found themselves 0-1 up with a goal from a free kick by Francis Cassidy. In the 40th minute Micky Banton made it 0-2 to the away Club. In the second half Aylesbury came back with a goal from Glen Donegal but Chesham held out to win the match 1-2.

In between the Loctite Cup games Chesham played Worthing FC in the league, a game they needed to win to secure the championship. Byron Walton scored the opening goal in this game. Dawber scored two, Goldstone from a penalty, Banton got one and Bateman put away a hat trick to put the finishing touches to a marvellous season for the Club in the league.

Chesham United had won the Vauxhall Football League division one championship, the highest the Club had ever been in its history. This was achieved with a record 102 goals. The Club were now in the mood for the return game against Aylesbury in the second leg of the Loctite Cup. The return leg turned out to be a true Cup tie classic with both teams playing end to end football. It was Aylesbury who got the first goal in the 35th minute when ex-Chesham player Dave Sansom put them ahead and when half time arrive the score was still 0-1 to the visitors.

In the second half the home Club put the pressure on Aylesbury and in the 66th minute the goal came that put Chesham into the final, a cross came over and found the head of Micky Barnes who made no mistake and put the ball firmly in the back of the net. The full time score was 1-1 and 3-2 to Chesham on aggregate. George Borg's players had done it again, with another top premier club defeated and a cup final to come on 8 May.

The last few league games were played out with a 0-0 draw at home to Walton and Hersham and a 0-3 away win at Dorking FC. In the last league game played, Met-Police who were to be relegated came to the Meadow and turned the tables on Chesham with a 1-3 win. The home Club put up little resistance in a very poor game and it showed that the Cup Final was on their minds.

The final of the Loctite Cup was played on Wednesday 8 May at Hendon's ground. Premier League club Bishops Stortford had reached the final after coming from behind to beat Redbridge Forest in the other semi-final. Chesham put up an excellent performance in the first half and it was a classic Gary Attrell goal on the 37th minute that put Chesham 1-0 up by half-time. Cheered on by large Chesham support, Chesham kept up the pressure in the second half, and it was a very rare mistake by Billy Goldstone that allowed Bishops to draw level in the 57th minute, when Pat Ryan made the score 1-1. Again Chesham took the lead when Dawber squeezed the ball home from a very tight angle. Soon afterwards Risley had put Bishops on level terms again, this time latching into a long throw in the 70th minute.

Dawber was pulled down in the penalty box, and to everyone's surprise was not awarded a penalty. The full time score was 2-2, and extra time was played. The nearest Chesham came to scoring again was a Walton header which just went over the bar. So after extra time both teams had to go to a penalty shoot out. The winning team was Bishops after their captain Hopkins scored and Chesham's May had missed. Bishops Stortford had won 5-4 on penalties.

1991-92 season

Chesham United's first season in the Premier Division was a challenge for everyone connected to the Club. A new drainage system was put into the playing surface before the start of the season. The Club had never reached this level before, but last season's results against Premier clubs showed that Chesham could more than hold their own against them.

George Borg's hopes were to maintain the same squad of players and with just a few new names he did just that. New signings included Justin Beacher from Chelmsford City, Andy Adebowale and Pat Ryan both from Bishops Stortford. Both had played against Chesham in the Loctite Cup. Steve Bateman signed a new contract and Keith Power became the Club's fitness trainer. Barbara McGowan took the post of Club Secretary.

George Borg was having talks with mini-football co-ordinator Graham Spittles in the hope of encouraging youngsters to form the back bone of the clubs future. Even the Isthmian league took on a new look with the link up with International sportswear company Diadora. The league's new title would be the Diadora League and this included the Premier Division, divisions one, two and three. The new sponsorship was in the region of £400,000 over three years and was the largest sponsorship deal in the pyramid structure. Chesham's rewards for the last season were £2,500 for the championship, £529.12 a share of the four goal victory, and £1,400 as runners up in the Loctite Cup. Warren May's miss in the penalty shoot out cost the Club £600. George Borg received two manager of the month awards in November and April with a pay out of £500, this made a total of £4,929.12.

The Club's pre-season games were against Reading, Barnet, Brentford and Dunstable. In the first of these games Reading FC came to the Meadow on 27 July. Chesham held their senior opponents to a 0-0 draw in a very entertaining game. On 31 July Barnet paid the Meadow a visit. Barnet had just won promotion into the Football League so the fans were looking forward to a good display of football.

Barnet arrived with a good squad of players including first team players Nugent, Hoddle, Bull and Naylor. Unfortunately Barnet did not get the result as Chesham ran out 1-0 winners with Michael Banton getting the goal. Dunstable had a visit from Chesham in another friendly with the away Club scoring 0-4. Mauling, Walton and Bateman got the goals. The real test came when Brentford came to the Meadow Park.

The Meadow in 1991 when 'A' grading for the ground was achieved

Brentford's team included top goal scorers Gary Blissett and Richard Cadette. In a very entertaining game with lots of goals, Brentford were 1-3 up by half time. When the final whistle had gone Chesham had pulled the score back to 3-4 after a late revival.

Chesham's league campaign started with an away game against Grays Athletic. The team for the first game in the Premier League was Walton, Goldstone, Ryan, May, Barnes, Bateman, Dawber, Adebowale, Banton, Mitchell, and Norman, with substitutes Cosby and Attrell.

It turned out to be an excellent start with a 1-3 win. Bateman scored twice and Banton once. The following Tuesday another away win was achieved this time against local rivals Aylesbury. Lomas came back into goal to replace Walton and Cosby changed places with Dawber on the subs bench. In front of 1,318 fans Chesham showed real class and determination by winning 1-2. Bateman scored again and an own goal caused Aylesbury's downfall. Chesham's first home game was billed as a cracker against the league favourites Woking. In front of 1,299 fans for much of the game Chesham outclassed the away team and in the end the points were shared in an 0-0 draw.

The first home win in the league was against Bishops Stortford and revenge was sweet for the defeat in the Loctite Cup. The result was 2-1, Attrell and Mitchell getting the goals. By September Chesham had a very healthy position in the league. In Cup competitions Tooting and Mitcham held Chesham to a 2-2 draw at the Meadow, Chesham winning the replay 2-3. A 3-0 win against Marlow pushed Chesham into third place one point behind the leaders Kingstonian. Wolverton came to the Meadow in the preliminary round of the FA Cup on 14 September. Chesham ran out 5-1 winners.

By this time new signing Lee Costa, who made his debut at home to Tooting and Mitcham, was making the midfield buzz. Lee had come from the Manchester camp. In the same month Tamworth came to play Chesham in the Trophy first qualifying round. Man of the match was Mark Dawber. He also got the winner as the home Club won 1-0. In the early part of October it was announced that MFI were to link up as main sponsors to Chesham United in a major sponsorship deal. This was one of a few sponsorship deals involving a major company within non-league football.

The FA Cup second qualifying round took Chesham to Vicarage Road, home of Watford and Wealdstone. Chesham's team work was very exciting and in the end they ran out 2-4 winners with Cosby, Ryan, Goldstone (penalty) and Banton, scoring the goals. In the next round a 2-2 draw at Brimsdown Rovers meant a replay at the Meadow, 585 fans watched as Chesham won 2-1. Chesham's next round was away to Aylesbury the old rivals.

The return match at the Meadow in front of 1,504 fans saw Aylesbury win 1-3 after a poor night and thus ended a good Cup run. Two defeats and a draw in the league saw Chesham slip from third to seventh. It was in the League Cup that some form came back with a 0-1 away win at Staines Town. Nugent on loan from Barnet got the goal. A 1-1 draw away to Sutton United saw Andy Lomas injured yet again with two broken fingers, and again Steve Bateman took his place in goal. Lomas would be out for six weeks with his injury, a period seeing many changes at the Club.

Mark Jones the commercial manager made his exit and in came Jim Halley with the new title of Business Development Manager. The third qualifying round of the Trophy saw Chesham away to Burton Albion. Both teams played attacking football with chances going to both sides. The result was a 0-0 draw and a replay at the Meadow. The replay turned out to be a one sided affair with the home Club winning 4-0, Richardson and Gipp getting two each.

In the league Chesham's performance away to Bishops Stortford in a 0-0 draw showed that George Borg was struggling to get things right. Six league games without a win proved to be George's downfall. It was just before the home game to Bognor Regis on 11 December that the

Club announced the departure of George Borg. He came to the Club with a good pedigree and left with a even better one. Once again Dave Brown took over as caretaker manager and a run of five defeats from six games saw Chesham's form slump.

In the Trophy on 11 January Chesham made the long trip to Yeovil and their new stadium. In front of 1,773 fans Yeovil ran out 1-3 winners. Buckingham were knocked out of the Berks & Bucks Senior Cup at the Meadow. Barnes, Richardson, Banton and Ryan all scoring.

Chesham travelled to Woking on 18 January as complete underdogs. Woking's support had been amazing all season and this match was no exception with a gate of over 2,300. Chesham took the lead with Banton scoring. Late into the second half Woking equalised then added the winner.

In contrast only 50 turned out at Leyton Wingate to see Chesham win 4-0 in the Loctite Cup. Unrest amongst the players over the Borg sacking meant that changes took place within the team. Dell, Angell, Vowles, York, Rake, Townsend and Costa all came into the squad over the past few months.

On 11 February Slough Town played Chesham at the Meadow in the Berks & Bucks Senior Cup. This match also saw the launch of the new look programme. Chesham's new look team for this game was Lomas, Vowles, Norman, York, Bateman, Goldstone, Rake, Abedowale, Richardson, Mitchell, and Attrell. To everyone's surprise the very inconsistent Chesham United put up one of their best displays all season to beat their senior opponents 3-1, goals coming twice from the very much improved Mitchell and Richardson, to ensure a semi-final away game with Aylesbury on 17 March.

In the quarter final of the Loctite Cup, Chesham were at home to Woking and the goal keeper jinx struck again. Chesham took the lead with Mitchell getting the goal, but soon after this Bateman had to take the place of Lomas. With this substitution went Chesham's chances of progressing as Woking ran out 2-5 winners. Mitchell had sustained a very bad knee injury in the away league game to Wokingham Town. This was to keep him out well over a season, a big blow to the Club as Mitchell was improving all the time. In the league Chesham held 11th position on 17 March.

The game many fans were waiting to see finally arrived, the semi-final of the Berks & Bucks Cup away to Aylesbury. A few Chesham players were carrying injuries including goal keeper Lomas. This meant a stand in goalkeeper, Walton was one of the subs. The Chesham team was Lomas, Goldstone, York, Vowles, Barnes, Bateman, Rake, Abedowale, Richardson, Dawber, and Attrell, with subs Banton and Walton. At half time the score was 0-0. In the 57th minute Aylesbury took the lead when Sansom scored from a rebound in a crowded goal mouth.

Chesham came back in fine style with Attrell making it 1-1 from the penalty spot in the 64th minute after Richardson was bought down. Chesham got the winner when Goldstone found Bateman's head from a free kick, leaving the final score line 1-2 to Chesham, who would meet Windsor and Eton in the final at Abingdon.

In the weeks that followed the Club announced the appointment of Gerald Aplin as the new manager, along with Alan Randall and Micky Gilchrist. On a evening that resembled a snow storm in the Antarctic, Chesham played Harrow at home in the league. Chesham's former manager George Borg was the manager of Harrow and the team also contained a number of former Chesham players. Six players that used to play for Chesham played in this match and Chesham were lucky to get three points from this game especially when Gipp missed a penalty for Harrow. Chesham won 1-0 with a goal from Barnes.

With a good run in the league over that last few games Chesham's league position improved and they finished fourth behind Sutton on goal difference. Gerald Aplin won manager of the month award for April with eight wins from ten games. Micky Barnes was named Chesham

United's player of the year and Gary Attrell won the player's player of the year. The sad point of the season was the loss of Charlie Rogers. Charlie had been a very keen supporter of the Club for over thirty years and had served on many committees.

On 25 April three coaches of supporters travelled to Abingdon for the Berks & Bucks Cup Final against Windsor and Eton. Chesham's support totalled over a thousand. Chesham's team were Lomas, Goldstone, York, Townsend, Barnes, Bateman, Rake, Adebowale, Richardson, Dawber, and Attrell. Banton substituted for Townsend, Davies not used. Chesham completely dominated the match and won the Cup for the first time since 1976. The final score was 5-1 with goals from Dawber (penalty) Adebowale, Bateman, Attrell, and Banton. Windsor's goal came from Leroy Messitt. Chesham had met the challenge in fine style in the Premier league and won the Senior County Cup.

1992-93 season
At each home game during the season Chesham ran onto the pitch to Tina Turner's "Simply the Best", and it is true to say this was the best. A big star Mark Lawrenson joined during the close season. Ex-Liverpool, and Republic of Ireland, he had been playing for Corby Town. Chelsea midfield player Robin Thomas also joined.

Pre-season friendlies included games against Brentford, Watford, Farnborough, Chelsea, Queens Park Rangers, Beaconsfield and Abergavenny Thursdays. The first of these games saw newly appointed Brentford at Meadow Park, Chesham holding them to a 2-2 draw. Brentford's team included Rostron and Blissett.

Chesham's squad were, Lomas, York, Vowles, Bateman, Barnes, Thomas, Rake, Adebowale, Townsend, Dawber, and Attrell. In the second half Walton, Davies, Bashir, Goldstone, Hamlett, Richardson, and Banton all played. Most of the players were lucky to escape a lightning storm a few days before while training. Even so Richardson, Attrell, Dawber and Rake were all affected by this.

On 29 July a Watford side played at the Meadow. The away team won 0-1 when Paul Vowles got in the way of a rebound and scored an own goal. Chesham travelled to Abergavenny Thursday in Wales the following Saturday. In this friendly, Micky Barnes broke his jaw and missed a few games. Chesham won 0-1.

Farnborough Town gave Chesham a good game on 4 August with the home team winning 4-3. During this time Naseem Bashir signed for the Club. The next game was away to Beaconsfield. Mark Lawrenson played his first full game for Chesham and they won 2-3.

The last game before the league started was against QPR, when Chesham put in a fine performance ending in a 3-2 win.

The league started with an away to Hendon, the favourites to win the league. Chesham's team were Lomas, Goldstone, York, Bateman, Costa, Rake, Adebowale, Richardson, Townsend, and Davies. With Chesham on top for most of the game Hendon still managed to get three points with their 2-1 win a blow to Chesham after the pre-season games.

The next few league games resulted in a 0-4 win away at Wivenhoe, a 3-1 home win with Wokingham Town, a 2-1 home win with Basingstoke Town, and a 0-3 away win at Harrow Borough. These set Chesham up in the league with one of the Club's longest unbeaten runs, of 18 wins and 5 draws. This total of 23 games without defeat saw the Club rise to the top of the league.

The run ended with a defeat to Stevenage Borough on 6 February 1993. In the FA Cup a crushing 9-1 home win against Boreham Wood after a 2-2 draw saw the Club facing Molesey in the next round and yet another win, this time 0-4. Berkhamsted Town were next and Chesham

Chesham United 1992-1993

won 3-0 at home. Mark Lawrenson was making his first team appearance. Mark received a fax from his old friend Kenny Dalglish before this game wishing him all the best.

Chesham's run in the FA Cup came to an end with an away defeat by Solihull Borough 3-1. Leyton put Chesham out of the League Cup with a 2-1 win, and another Leighton, Leighton Town, knocked Chesham out of the Buckingham Charity Cup 3-1. Stevenage Borough won 1-3 at the Meadow in the Full Members Cup.

It was in the Trophy that Chesham had the most success. Before the game against Leicester United, Chesham had a big test in the league home from close rivals St Albans. Chesham's recent wins were 7-1 against Stevenage Borough, 6-1 against Bognor Regis, and a very impressive 5-1 home win against Carshalton Athletic, who were in the top five. The Chesham team that took the field against St Albans in front of 1,456 supporters were Lomas, York, Coleman, Bateman, Barnes, Casta, Rake, Adebowale, Bashir, Townsend, and Attrell, with subs Davies and Dawber. The result was a 2-2 draw and this put Chesham 13 points clear of Enfield.

Bromley put the skids on Chesham's goal spree with another 2-2 draw. This turned out to be Mark Lawrenson's last game for Chesham. Chesham came back with vengeance in the Trophy against Leicester United winning 7-3, including a hat trick for Townsend. Club Captain Steve Bateman received his Diadora league representative cap just before this game and it was also announced that Chesham manager Gerald Aplin had won the manager of the month award for the second month. Gary Attrell scored a glorious goal from a free kick in Chesham's 3-2 win over Grays Athletic in the league. Grays had the old Chesham favourite, Billy Goldstone, playing for them. Billy scored for Grays to make the score 2-2 before Gary Attrell struck.

In the next round of the Trophy, Rugby were beaten 6-1 on their own ground. Chesham's reputation for scoring goals was now growing. Newbury Town were knocked out of the Berks & Bucks Cup by 2-1 at the Meadow. The next round of the Trophy was sure to be a classic, Dover Athletic top of the Beazer Homes Premier League against Chesham United top of the Diadora Premier League at the Meadow. Chesham's line up for this game Lomas, York, Bashir, Bateman, Barnes, Cobb, Coleman, Rake, Banton, Townsend, and Attrell with subs Richardson and Dawber. Gary Cobb made his home debut for Chesham. The gate for this game was 2,055. Chesham played a tight and professional game and as a result Darren Coleman scored the all important goal in the 36th minute. In the second half Dover really came at Chesham and tough tactics were the order of the day. York was unfairly tackled and spent most of the match limping, Micky Barnes had his nose broken but was determined to play out the 45 minutes. Chesham held on to a very well deserved 1-0 victory and a quarter final game at home to Sutton United. The Berks & Bucks Cup saw Chesham away to old rivals Windsor and Eton, who were much financial trouble. The league was getting a little close with Chesham's lead being reduced to one point after a poor display away to Stevenage Borough ending the Club's long run without defeat. The Club still pushing Chesham were St Albans with their top scorers Clark and Williams keeping them in the frame. A very good match was to take place between the two in the league at Clarence Park on 13 February. Chesham were back to full strength for this game after having many injuries over the last few months. 3,120 fans came to watch the two teams battle it out the biggest gate of the season in the Diadora League.

Once again Chesham were on top for most of the first half but the score remained 0-0. In the second half Townsend managed to put Chesham in front but St Albans soon came back to make the score 1-1 with Clark getting the goal. The final score was 1-1 in a very fine game between two very good teams. On 20 February Sutton United played Chesham in the next round of the Trophy. Over 1,500 supporters turned up for this match expecting to see Chesham win, but Sutton who started as underdogs ran out 1-3 winners with Banton scoring the Chesham goal.

One of the most exciting games in the league took place when Chesham were at home to Marlow on 27 February. The final score was 4-3 to the home Club but the game had plenty to keep the fans on their toes for the full 90 minutes. Each side had two penalties with Costa, twice, Barnes and Townsend scoring for Chesham.

Dave Webley made his debut for Chesham in the Marlow game. A Welsh semi-pro he had played for Merthyr Tydfil and Inter-Cardiff before joining Chesham. Chesham continued to do well in the league and by the end of March they had opened up a small gap.

From 24 February to 31 March Chesham played 9 and won 9, with 30 goals for and just 4 against. The team were giving good value for money and well on the way to the Premier Championship. The final of the Berks & Bucks Cup was reached for the second season when Chesham defeated Flackwell Heath in the semi-final 0-4. The final itself was held at Aylesbury against Abingdon Town from Division One of the Diadora League on 17 April. A few days before the final the Club announced in its programme and the local press that promotion to the G M Vauxhall Conference league would not take place even if the championship was won. The Conference made it clear that the ground was not up to the required standards laid down in its rules, and thousands of pounds of work were needed in a short period of time to rectify the situation. The board felt this was impossible, The decision did not seem to affect the team as they still maintained their form. Chesham United's second successive Senior Cup final was secured by Chris Townsend who scored the winning goal in a 1-0 triumph.

St Albans just beat Chesham to the 100 goal mark by seconds on the same day in the league. With a 0-0 draw at home against Bromley the championship was virtually Chesham's. In the last league game at home to Dulwich Hamlet Chesham had to lose 3-0 and St Albans had to win 10-0 at home to Sutton. In the end Chesham put in a performance of champions and won 4-0, St Albans drew 2-2, and Chesham United were Diadora Premier League Champions in just two seasons of being in the Premier League. Micky Barnes was voted the supporters' "Player of the Year". The last game of the season was a friendly against a full strength Chelsea team. This game was to launch the ground improvement fund C.U.B.A. Chesham showed the fans why they were champions with a superb display of football and won 4-1.

CHAPTER 11

Chesham's Renaissance 1993-98

1993-94 season

July's pre-season games saw a 3-3 draw with Southend, and victories over Crystal Palace 2-1 and Norwich 3-1. The season's opener was a 3-2 win over Yeading.

On 7 September Chesham won the Isthmian League Charity Shield beating Marlow 4-1 at home. Sebastian Coe presented the Shield.

Dave Beasant, FA Cup hero of 1988, was on hand to present the man of the match award for the home tie with Wivenhoe Town which Chesham won 5-1.

The season's FA Cup run ended at home to Kidderminister Town 4-1. CUBA, Chesham's fund raising arm announced they needed some £60-70,000 to bring the ground up to Conference standard. Mickey Barnes and Steve Bateman were selected for the Diadora League representative side. Steve Bateman received his cap for 5 Isthmian appearances in his career. Trevor Brooking and Tommy Docherty both visited the Chess suite for Gentlemen's' Dinners. Christmas saw the local council give the thumbs down to assisting Chesham's Conference bid.

Keith Power was hired as fitness coach. A 8-0 win over Beaconsfield United in the Berks & Bucks Cup set Chesham up for a shot at the silver ware.

In January 1994 Peter Gibbins resigned as a Club Director because of work pressures. England failed to reach the World Cup in the USA. Gerald Aplin resigned and Alan Randall took over as manager. On 22 May, Chesham were defeated by Marlow 1-0 with a David Lay goal in the Berks & Bucks final at Elm Park Reading.

At the end of the season the Club went into limbo. The Club had been offered for sale in the national newspapers in March 1994, but there were no takers.

1994-95 season

The Club's saviours were two local businessmen, Dennis Bone and David Pembroke, who agreed to take over the running of the Club until a financial solution could be devised. On 17 June 1994, they took over the running of Chesham United from Tony Aplin, Robert Old, and Jess Conrad. Bill Wells stayed on as Club President.

Their problems in mid July 1994 were enormous, no manager, five contract players only, four of whom wanted to leave, a pitch that had been left to the summer growth. Paul Roberts who came straight from league football at Colchester became player -manager and was able to put together a team that included ex-West Ham and Chelsea star Alan Dickens. Bob Pearson ex-Millwall manager became the new Director of football. Millwall FC linked up with Chesham to give their developing players the opportunity of games at a lower level, with obvious benefits to both clubs.

A financial solution was trashed out by late September and David Pembroke became the major shareholder and Chairman. New faces appeared on the Club's board. They were Nick Wells, Len Vockins, Ken Ambrose and Ron Champion.

Apart from a good run in the FA Cup with victories over Conference sides Dagenham and Bromsgrove the performances on the pitch became a struggle and in January 1995, Jim Kelman took over from Paul Roberts in the manager's chair.

Although it came to the last game before the inevitable was confirmed, Chesham were relegated back to Division One, a sad day for the Club and Town.

Alan Dickens

Icis, the Chesham based sports firm paid half a million pounds to sponsor the league for the season 1995-96. Stanley Matthews kicked off Eddie Bailey's testimonial match which pitted an old Chesham XI team with an old Spurs XI.

1995-96 season
A home friendly with Slough Town and a 1-0 win gave an encouraging start to the season. Ex-Spurs, ex-Reading star Stewart Beavon scored the Club's opening league goal to give a 2-1 victory over Thame.

USA World Cup star, John Kerr, signed to play a half season between international duties. He became a big hit scoring some spectacular goals. Brackley Town star, John "Bomber" Blencoe signed on. His chief claim to fame is as an old school mate of mine.

Syd McDonnell was made the Club's First Life Vice-President. £15,000 spent on ground improvements. The Club's accounts showed a £5,000 profit. Gate money decreased by £33,000 because of last season's relegation. 26 January saw the departure of Jim Kelman and Paul O'Reilly took over the reins. Chesham finished 12th in Division One.

1996-1997 season
Watford reserves used the Meadow for their home fixtures. Micky Barnes announced his retirement at 33 years old. An August friendly with Watford was lost 2-0 with David Connelly, the Irish International scoring the opener. On 6 September 1996 Rebecca Pembroke led the friends of Chesham Charity walk and £500 was raised.

Chesham United's oldest supporter Herbie Wallace died aged 89. October bought honours for leading goal scorer of the month, John Lawford with October's and November's manager of the month awards going to Paul O'Reilly. In March Paul O'Reilly was replaced by Andy Thomas as manager. This ex-Oxford and Newcastle star retired due to injury and became manager of the season. Ron Lee and Jim Chambers joined the Club's board.

Chesham United 1996-1997 in their new away strip

MFI unveiled new kit in their corporate colours of orange and dark blue. On 18 April 1997 Chesham topped the Division One table. The season's highlight was on 4 May when a home 2-1 win over second place Basingstoke Town clinched promotion and the title.

Chesham United 1997-1998

CHAPTER 12

Youth and Women's Football

The Youth Team

The Youth Team was reformed in 1994-95 by Nick Wells, the then Chiltern Athletic U16's manager, and Phil Devlin, of Missenden Juniors U16's. The initial squad was based on the players from those two teams and that season was spent playing friendlies, most notably against Millwall.

The Club entered the Youth Team in the Allied Counties Youth League the following season. This is a high standard league comprised mainly of the major non-league clubs in the South of England, together with a number of professional clubs, Oxford United, Wycombe Wanderers and Reading. It was a young side and Chesham took time to settle at this higher standard. By Christmas however the team had begun to find its feet and finished the season in a respectable position in the lower half of the table. One of the high points of the season was Andy Reeder signing a contract with the first team.

In 1996-97 the Youth team proved to be a better cup side than league side, reaching the semi-finals of the Berks & Bucks Youth Cup, losing to Abingdon Town, and the quarter finals of the Allied Counties League Cup, losing to Hillingdon Borough, but finishing only 9th out of 12 in the league. Nevertheless, a number of players began to catch the eye, most notably Will Miles whose promising first team debut against Enfield in the Full Members Cup was rewarded with a contract.

The 1997-98 season has seen a reserve team being re-established at Chesham United, managed by Nick Wells. A flourishing reserve side is an essential part of any youth policy, providing the link between the Youth and First Teams. Phil Devlin continues as Manager of the Youth team, which was beginning to reap the rewards of the previous three years hard work. At Christmas 1997 the team was neck and neck with Maidenhead United at the top of the league and has only

Chesham United Youth Football Club

been beaten once by Hornchurch in the FA Youth Cup. The Team is also in the quarter finals of the Berks & Bucks Youth Cup, scoring 34 goals and conceding none on the way. The team contains a large number of very promising players, of whom the Club has high hopes. Mark Welling made an impressive debut for the first team earlier this season against Gravesend and Northfleet in the Full Members Cup, and Rob Eade has currently progressed to the final 30 players trial for the England Schools' squad.

Bill Power, to whom this Chapter is dedicated

The Juniors
Setting up a full club infrastructure must be the ambition of all clubs. After the 1990 World Cup in Italy a football administrator was appointed with the objective of creating several junior pyramids in the south of England. The Club's Directors at the time were agreeable to introducing juniors to Chesham. The idea had been brought to the Club by Mickey Clark, on a commission basis.

In 1992 a break away group led by Bill Power, sadly no longer with us, set up Chesham United Youth FC as what it is today. Bill Power became its secretary, Graham Spittles Treasurer, and Chris Morris Chairman. The Club was initially based on 6-9 year olds in three bands of ability. It plays on the Meadow, and at Thomas Harding School from March to November on quarter size pitches. The Club's biggest cost remains pitch hire. With no grants available it remains self funding.

In 1992 the 11-a-side under 10s started with a place in the Wycombe and South Bucks Star league with 20 to 30 boys in the squad. Now the Club has some 400 signed on. Many parents help as referees in matches up to under 15, when allocated referees are appointed. There are 18 boys in every age group from under 10s to under 16. All abilities are encouraged, and everybody joins in.

Bill Power set up junior football to encourage friendship, fair play and sportsmanship. The continuing success of his creation is surely the best way of recording his vision.

Chesham United Ladies' FC
This the newest section of the Club was formed in 1995 through the efforts of Tracey Cook and Vanessa Hardwick, two local girls whose interest in Chesham arose after the closure of Marlow FC. The section caters for the ever increasing local interest in playing football amongst young ladies in the 17-35 age range. Based at the Meadow, where most home matches are played, the team is managed by Paul Huntly and Robert Bristow. The 16 player squad train regularly and have achieved much local praise.

Chesham United Ladies' Football Club

Moor Ladies 1920 – possibly the oldest-known picture of a Ladies' Football team

CHAPTER 13

The Supporters' Club

Chesham United Football Supporters' Club was founded in 1936. The earliest records go back to an AGM held in June 1938, when its President was Mr M Lucas, Chairman Mr G Barnes, Honorary Treasurer Mr A J Tree and Honorary Secretary Mr H W White.

During that year terracing had been built on the popular side, the stands were painted and £79 was given to the Club. Membership stood at 438. The Club was disbanded at the outbreak of the war in September 1939.

On 11 September 1945, a special meeting was held to consider restarting the Supporters' Club. Mr Tommy Stillman took the chair for the meeting and it was agreed to restart the Club and a committee was formed.

During the 1950-51 season a new stand was erected on the popular side, named the Tommy Stillman stand. More terracing was laid on the same side, and at the AGM of that year the Club's assets totalled £591 and the membership stood at 460. The official handing over of the stand took place on 25 August 1951. Total donations to the Club from 1951-56 were £1,253 plus £633 paid out for ground improvements, including the cost of bringing electricity to the ground in 1957.

On 22 September 1964 the Club switched on their new floodlights, the Supporters' Club having raised approximately one-third of the total cost. The expansion of the Clubhouse was the brain child of Mr Leo Chittenden, who was undeterred by the Club's poverty stricken position with debts always on the doorstep. With a few other faithful friends of the Club and a gift of £600 from the Supporters' Club it was made possible. Building started during the summer of 1958. Mr Jack Keen, the local builder had a deadline to complete the work before the start of the season even though he had very few fine working days. The clubhouse was finished on time and opened by the Chairman of the Council.

When the main stand burnt down in 1983, the extent of the damage was in the region of £50,000. The Club really needed its supporters. The extra money needed to build a new stand was £20,000, and this was found by asking the supporters to come forward as guarantors on a bank loan. For eight months the bank did not receive payments on the loan, because league regulations concerning safety prevented games being played at the Meadow during this period. Consequently the bank decided to call in the loan from the guarantors and this £20,000 saved the Club from liquidation.

During the early part of 1990-91 the Directors of the Club decided to disband the Supporters' Club. Funds of £5,000 were handed over to the Club. Match day committees helped run the Club on a voluntary basis. The Club Shop was run by Club Shop manager Mr R Day. In 1992-93 season the Club Shop had its own sponsor, the first time of its kind. The takings during the championship season were £3,000. £300 being taken on one match day, not bad for one small shop.

In the modern game there is more pressure on the supporter to generate more funds. These are needed not just to run the Club but also to help pay the high wages that players demand. Chesham United over the years has had some fantastic support. Even back in the 1920's the support was in the 2,000 region. In 1921 when Chesham played Slough at Maidenhead in the semi-final of the Berks & Bucks Cup over 3,000 fans attended. In September 1921, 1,200 fans turned up to the match to open the new stand.

In a FA game against Botwell Mission of Hayes in October 1921 Chesham's gate was 2,500. A home game against Oxford City again in the FA Cup produced 5,000 spectators on 10

November 1922. The Berks & Bucks Cup final in 1922 against Wycombe Wanderers drew 6,000. 1929's Berks & Bucks Cup final at Loakes Park brought in 10,000, and in the third round of the FA Cup against Cambridge in 1979-80, 5,000 packed into the Meadow.

Of course the largest support was attracted to the FA Amateur Cup final of 1968. A total of 28,400 saw Chesham play 16 games to get to the final. 8,000 turned up to see the semi-final against Wealdstone at Fulham FC at a time when Chesham's population was 20,000. 5,000 supporters crammed into the Broadway to welcome the team home from Wembley.

Chesham have been lucky to have had a very loyal band of supporters over the years, and to continue to enjoy their support, when many clubs have failed through of the lack of support. Gates may be lower these days because of fans have other interests but Chesham's gates are as good as any other Conference club, and their main sponsorship is the envy of many.

Chesham United Supporters' Club

CHAPTER 14

The Best of Chesham

George Barnes

George was born in 1899 and died in 1961. His involvement with the Club was as player, President, Committee member and crucially as the employer of many of the other players. The success of the Britannia Boot Company and the death of George Barnes senior meant that his football career was at times limited. His successes at Watford FC are still remembered and the performances of this exceptionally talented outside left shone out in Berks & Bucks sides dominated by Wycombe players.

The War put paid to his playing career. George was highly thought of, not only for his efforts in making the Club a force to be reckoned with, but for his whole hearted approach to all its dealings. He was particularly active in finding unemployed players work, often in his own business. His enjoyment of all sports was evident, he loved his golf and bowls. He won many cups and trophies for the Club, for example captaining the successful side in 1922 which bagged six trophies that season. In service George Barnes served in the Royal Engineers based in Suffolk at Bungay as a dispatch rider.

George Barnes (right, middle row) Club Captain through the successful 1920s

Syd MacDonnell

Syd MacDonnell was a devoted supporter and acted as Club Administrator through the Club's highs and lows. Born and bred in Chesham man Syd attended Germain Street school leaving at 14. Like many local people he worked for George Barnes' Boot factory, where he played junior soccer as a right winger and joined the local unit of the territorial army. Called up a week before the Second World War, Syd served as an instructor with the 2nd Bucks Infantry before being posting to the 6th Royal Scots Infantry. But Syd's part in the war ended on 8 July 1944 aged just

22. Wriggling through the slit trenches in the hill above Caen, a bomb exploded blowing off his right leg just below the knee, smashing his left leg to a pulp and inflicting a double compound fracture to his right arm. But Sgt MacDonnell 5385016 did not give up, regaining consciousness a week later in Southampton Military Hospital.

Syd Macdonnell

For many years Syd was President of the Chesham Sunday League, CUFC Supporters' Club and later Director and Secretary of the Club.

John Pratt

Born June 26 1948 in Hackney. Through Chesham's difficult times John had very limited success, but as a manager his professionalism and coaching will be remembered for many a year. He signed schoolboy forms in November 1965 and his career at Spurs spanned 1968 - 1980, where his honours included the UEFA Cup 1971-72, and the League Cup 1972-73. He played 381 games, scoring 49 goals for Tottenham.

John Pratt

Steve Bateman
Born in 1964 in Berkhamsted, Steve was not only a talented footballer also showed fine style as a cricketer. After being rejected by Howard Kendall at Everton after skippering a successful youth side at Goodison Park, Steve resumed his career in amateur and semi-professional football with Harrow in 1989 before joining Chesham and leading them to some of the Club's most successful times. Steve not only won County Cup honours but also Premier Championships. Individual honours came with an Isthmian League cap, Herts County, Middlesex XI and FA XI representations. His partnership with Mickey Barnes at the heart of a solid defence was the envy of non-league football for several seasons.

Tommy Langley
Born in London on 8 February 1958, he signed professional forms for Chelsea in March 1975, making his debut earlier in November 1974 against Leicester City. He had 139 appearances, scoring 43 goals for Chelsea. His playing career included spells at QPR, Crystal Palace, AEK Athens, Coventry City, Wolves, Aldershot, and Exeter. A former England Youth international he had 20 appearances for Chesham.

Mark Lawrenson
Bob Paisley broke Liverpool's transfer record to sign Mark from Brighton in August 1981 for £900,000. Rated world class in the mid 1980's and a host of achievements his career finished at the Meadow with 6 brief appearances prompting the BBC to run a standing room only profile on Mark. Born in Preston on 2 June 1957 he played 332 games for Liverpool scoring 17 goals. He was a member of the teams which won the European Cup 1983-84, the League Cup 1981-2, 1982-83, 1983-84, 1985-86, and 1987-88, and the FA Cup 1985-86. With 38 Republic of Ireland caps, he also played for Preston North End, Brighton and managed Oxford and Peterborough.

Alan Dickens
Born 3 September 1964, Alan had thirty appearances for Chesham. Costing West Ham £650,000, he appeared 192 times for them scoring 23 goals. His 15 appearances for Brentford added a further goal to his tally.

Tony Currie
This fine ex-Sheffield United and Leeds player with 34 England caps at all levels created a lot of media interest during his time with Chesham in 1983-84. The stand having been destroyed by fire, his home appearances were limited. His first appearance was away at Farnborough on 12 November 1993 in a 2-1 win. Shortly after leaving the club for Torquay, Les King received a letter from Tony thanking him for the fans' support during his short stay at the Meadow.

Martin Baguley
Martin was born on 8 November 1959 at Edgware and is affectionately nick-named "Baggers". He holds the Club record for appearances with over 600. His Club career started in the Club's reserve side and on impressive showings he graduated to the first team. Most of Martin's early football was played in the Watford area with Oxhey Jets. Aged 21, he made his Chesham debut away at Wokingham Town in 1979.

Mickey Barnes
Born Reading 17th September 1963, 6' 4". Pillar in defence. Joined Chesham in 1990 from Windsor via Barnet, Mickey formed a partnership with Steve Bateman at the centre of the defence for several seasons. The former England Youth and Isthmian League Representative player's career came to an abrupt end through injury in 1996.

The latest Programme Cover for the match against Stevenage Borough

Organised Football in Chesham

Chronology

1878	Berks & Bucks Footbal Association formed
1879	The first senior club in the Town started
1880	Chesham Cricket Club started
1887	Chesham Generals started
1894	Southern League founder members
1901	Berks & Bucks won by Generals
1902	Generals reach semi-final of FA Amateur Cup, lost 4-2 to the Old Malvernians
1903	Berks & Bucks won by Generals
1904	Berks & Bucks won by Town
	Senior League won by Generals
	Squire Lowndes dies
1905	Bucks & Berks Senior League - Generals runners up
1906	A police constable in attendance for every game
	Bucks & Berks Senior League - Town runners up
1908	Berks & Bucks won by Town
1909	Generals play in Spartan League until 1914
	Chesham Town win South Eastern League
1912	Athenian League founder members
1914	Generals win Spartan League
	Generals win Bucks Charity Cup
	Generals win Chesham Charity Cup
1917	Generals & Town amalgamated on 20 November
	Chesham United Football Club formed 1 December
1919	First game on Cricket Ground for Chesham United
	Generals wound up 22 November
1920	New stand built
	Berks & Bucks Charity Cup winners
1921	Supporters Club founded
1922	Berks & Bucks winners for the first time and Bucks Charity Cup
	Spartan League Division I and Division II winners
	Chesham Challenge Cup and Chesham District League winners
1923	Spartan League Division I winners
1925	Spartan League Division I winners
	Berks & Bucks Junior Cup winners
1926	Winners Spartan League Cup Winners Berks & Bucks
1927	Spartan League Division I runners up
1928	Won Berks & Bucks Junior Cup
1929	Berks & Bucks winners
	Chesham Sports Company founded
1930	Spartan League Premier Division runners up
1932	A new ground called "The Meadow" in September
	Won Berks & Bucks Junior Cup

1933	Spartan League Premier Division winners
1934	Berks & Bucks winners
	Spartan League Premier Division runners up
1939	William Frith Lowndes left Chesham and died
1947	Joined Corinthian League
1948	Berks & Bucks winners
	Won Junior Cup
1949	Worst defeat - 12-1 to Grays on 15 January
1951	Berks & Bucks winners
	Berks & Bucks Benevolence Cup winners
1961	Corinthian League runners up
	Winners of the Corinthian League Memorial Shield
1962	Corinthian League runners up
1963	Winners of the Corinthian League Memorial Shield
	Berks & Bucks Benevolence Cup Winners
	First Neale Trophy winners
	Record scorers with 80 goals - John Willis & Arthur Howlett
1964	Won Neale Trophy
	Won Memorial Shield - Athenian League Div I Runners up Reserves
	New floodlights used first against Luton 22 September
1965	Won Memorial Shield - Athenian League
	Berks & Bucks winners
1966	FA Cup 1st round v Enfield lost 5-0
1967	Berks & Bucks winners
	Sid Prosser left as manager 17 April. John Reardon becomes manager
1968	Runners up in the Amateur Cup final at Wembley on 20 April
	FA Cup 1st round v Colchester lost 0-5
1969	Corintian, Delphian & Athenian Leagues merge
	Win Corinthian League Memorial Shield
	FA Cup 1st round v Colchester
1970	Reserves runners up in Division 1
1971	Neale Trophy Winners
1972	Middlesex Border League champions Reserves
1976	FA Cup 1st round v Brentford lost 1-0
	Berks & Bucks winners
1980	5,000 attend FA Cup 3rd round v Cambridge lost 2-0
1983	Fire burnt down main stand 3 May
1984	Graham Taylor opens new stand 4 December
	St. Mary's Cup winners, Reserves win Apsley Senior Charity Cup
	Runners up Middlesex Borders League – Reserves
	Runners up AWA Cup
	Youth team win Servowarm Isthmian Cup
1985	Pat Morrissey sacked 11 March
1987	Centenary year-100 years of senior football in Chesham
	Won Isthmian League Division 2 - North in the Vauxhall Football League
	18 August - Arsenal 3-1
	29 August - Ground achieves "B" rating

1990	Ground "A" Rating achieved
1991	Runners up Loctite Cup, lost 5-4 on penalties to Bishops Stortford
	Winners Berks & Bucks Cup
	Winners Vauxhall League Division 1 with club record of 102 goals
1992	Chesham United Youth FC win Berks & Bucks Cup
1993	Winners Isthmian Premier Division (Diadora)
	Winners of Isthmian Charity shield presented by Seb Coe
	Berks & Bucks Cup
	GM Vauxhall Conference refused entry due to ground
1997	ICIS Division 1 winners

LEAGUE TABLES

1894-95 Southern League Division Two

		P	W	D	L	F	A	Pts
1	New Brompton	12	11	0	1	57	10	22
2	Sheppey United	12	6	1	5	25	23	13
3	Old St Stephens	12	6	0	6	26	26	12
4	Uxbridge	12	4	3	5	14	20	11
5	Bromley	12	4	1	7	23	30	9
6	**Chesham**	**12**	**3**	**3**	**6**	**20**	**42**	**9**
7	Maidenhead	12	2	4	6	19	33	8

1895-96 Southern League Division Two

		P	W	D	L	F	A	Pts
1	Wolverton L & NW Rly	16	13	1	2	43	10	27
2	Sheppey United	16	11	3	2	60	19	25
3	1st Scots Guards	16	8	5	3	37	22	21
4	Uxbridge	16	9	1	6	28	23	19
5	Old St Stephen's	16	6	3	7	34	21	15
6	Guildford	16	7	1	8	29	41	15
7	Maidenhead	16	4	1	11	20	49	9
8	**Chesham**	**16**	**2**	**3**	**11**	**15**	**48**	**7**
9	Bromley	16	2	2	12	16	49	6

1896-97 Southern League Division Two

		P	W	D	L	F	A	Pts
1	Dartford	24	18	4	4	83	19	38
2	Royal Engineers	24	11	9	4	49	37	31
3	Freemantle	24	12	4	8	58	40	28
4	Uxbridge	24	11	5	8	62	37	27
5	Wycombe Wanderers	24	10	6	8	37	54	26
6	**Chesham**	**24**	**11**	**3**	**10**	**41**	**55**	**25**
7	Southall	24	9	6	9	55	52	24
8	1st Scots Guards	24	9	6	9	49	50	24
9	Warmley (Bristol)	24	10	3	11	44	43	23
10	West Herts	24	11	1	12	41	49	23
11	Old St Stephen's	24	5	7	12	36	52	17
12	Maidenhead	24	4	8	12	33	64	18
13	1st Coldstream Guards	24	3	6	15	30	66	12

1897-98 Southern League Division Two

		P	W	D	L	F	A	Pts
1	Royal Artillery	22	19	1	2	75	22	39
2	Warmley (Bristol)	22	19	0	3	108	15	38
3	West Herts	22	11	6	5	50	48	28
4	Uxbridge	22	11	2	9	39	57	24
5	St Albans	22	9	5	8	47	41	23
6	Dartford	22	11	0	11	88	55	22
7	Southall	22	8	2	12	49	61	18
8	**Chesham**	**22**	**8**	**2**	**12**	**38**	**48**	**18**
9	Old St Stephen's	22	7	2	13	47	66	16
10	Wycombe Wanderers	22	7	2	13	37	55	16
11	Maidenhead	22	4	4	14	27	81	12
12	Royal Engineers	22	4	2	16	26	62	10

1898-99 Southern League Division Two

		P	W	D	L	F	A	Pts
1	Thames Ironworks	22	19	1	2	64	16	39
2	Wolverton	22	13	4	5	88	43	30
3	Watford	22	14	2	6	62	35	30
4	Brentford	22	11	3	8	59	39	25
5	Wycombe Wanderers	22	10	2	10	55	57	22
6	Southall	22	11	0	11	44	55	22
7	**Chesham**	**22**	**9**	**2**	**11**	**45**	**62**	**20**
8	St Albans	22	8	3	11	45	59	19
9	Shepherd's Bush	22	7	3	12	37	53	17
10	Fulham	22	6	4	12	36	44	16
11	Uxbridge	22	7	2	13	29	48	16
12	Maidenhead	22	3	2	17	33	86	8

1899-1900 Southern League Division Two

		P	W	D	L	F	A	Pts
1	Watford	20	14	2	4	56	25	30
2	Fulham	20	10	5	5	44	19	25
3	**Chesham Town**	**20**	**9**	**6**	**5**	**46**	**34**	**24**
4	Wolverton	20	11	2	7	43	38	24
5	Grays United	20	8	6	6	61	29	22
6	Shepherd's Bush	20	8	5	7	41	36	21
7	Wycombe Wanderers	20	8	3	9	35	50	19
8	Dartford	20	7	3	10	35	42	17
9	Brentford	20	5	7	8	31	48	17
10	Southhall	20	6	3	11	20	42	15
11	Maidenhead	20	2	2	16	18	84	6

1900-01 Southern League Division Two

		P	W	D	L	F	A	Pts
1	Brentford	16	14	2	0	63	11	30
2	Grays United	16	12	2	2	62	12	26
3	Sheppey United	16	8	1	7	44	26	17
4	Shepherd's Bush	16	8	1	7	30	30	17
5	Fulham	16	8	0	8	38	26	16
6	**Chesham Town**	**16**	**5**	**1**	**10**	**26**	**39**	**11**
7	Maidenhead	16	4	1	11	21	49	9
8	Wycombe Wanderers	16	4	1	11	23	68	9
9	Southall	16	4	1	11	22	68	9

1901-02 Southern League Division Two

		P	W	D	L	F	A	Pts
1	Fulham	16	13	0	3	51	19	26
2	Grays United	16	12	1	3	49	14	25
3	Brighton & Hove Albion	16	11	0	5	34	17	22
4	Wycombe Wanderers	16	7	3	6	36	30	17
5	West Hampstead	16	6	4	6	39	29	16
6	Sheperd's Bush	16	6	1	9	31	31	13
7	Southall	16	5	2	9	28	52	12
8	Maidenhead	16	3	1	12	23	59	7
9	**Chesham Town**	**16**	**2**	**2**	**12**	**24**	**64**	**6**

1902-03 Southern League Division Two

		P	W	D	L	F	A	Pts
1	Fulham	10	7	1	2	27	7	15
2	Brighton & Hove Albion	10	7	1	2	34	11	15
3	Grays United	10	7	0	3	28	12	14
4	Wycombe Wanderers	10	3	3	4	13	19	9
5	**Chesham Town**	**10**	**2**	**1**	**7**	**9**	**37**	**5**
6	Southall	10	1	0	9	10	35	2

1902-03 Berks & Bucks Senior League

		P	W	D	L	F	A	Pts
1	**Chesham Generals**	**10**	**6**	**2**	**2**	**27**	**15**	**14**
2	Aylesbury	10	5	2	3	36	21	12
3	Maidenhead North	10	4	3	3	16	15	11
4	Slough	10	4	2	4	17	20	10
5	Wycombe	10	3	3	4	19	28	9
6	Maidenhead	10	0	6	4	12	26	6

1903-04 Southern League-Division Two

		P	W	D	L	F	A	Pts
1	Watford	20	18	2	0	70	15	38
2	Portsmouth (Res.)	20	15	2	3	85	25	32
3	Millwall Athletic (Res.)	20	9	4	7	35	39	22
4	Southampton (Res.)	20	9	3	8	59	35	21
5	Grays United	20	9	3	8	25	55	21
6	Fulham (Res.)	20	8	4	8	40	34	20
7	Swindon Town (Res.)	20	8	3	9	50	44	19
8	Reading (Res.)	20	8	2	10	43	42	18
9	Wycombe Wanderers	20	5	5	10	29	64	15+
10	Southall	20	4	2	14	25	62	10
11	**Chesham Town**	**20**	**1**	**2**	**17**	**19**	**65**	**4**

1903-04 Berks & Bucks Senior League

		P	W	D	L	F	A	Pts
1	**Chesham Generals**	**10**	**7**	**2**	**1**	**20**	**4**	**16**
2	Aylesbury	10	7	1	2	31	14	13
3	Maidenhead North	10	5	2	3	15	10	12
4	**Chesham Town**	**10**	**4**	**2**	**4**	**16**	**19**	**10**
5	Slough	10	2	1	7	12	26	5
6	Maidenhead	10	0	2	8	5	26	2

Aylesbury had 2 points deducted this season.

John Watt
Long serving and a natural leader, John's experience helped the Club to some of its most successful times. Born in Airdrie on 23 November 1954, he was educated in High Wycombe at Hatters Lane School and played for Holtspur Minors. He joined Chesham in the 1969-70 season playing mainly Midweek Floodlit League matches before joining Watford, eventually signing a two year full professional contract under manager George Kirby, where his debut was away at Norwich City in the Second Division. He was selected by Scotland for final trials at Largs and played in the probables v possibles at Morton.

After several knee operations John returned to local football with Hayes and then Maidenhead. Returning to Chesham as Captain with Micky Hall in 1978 he lead the Club past seven non-league clubs to the meeting with Cambridge United in the FA Cup 3rd round which was lost 2-0 after John had hit the bar early on. John's subsequent career in management took him to Slough, Maidenhead, and Windsor and Eton, where John remained as coach.

Kerry Dixon
Kerry was born in Luton on 24 July 1961. His first memories of football come from his non league days at Chesham, where he was spotted and invited to become an apprentice at White Hart Lane. Kerry recollects: " obviously I jumped at the chance but when they asked me to become a full time professional, I refused because I wanted to complete my tool-making studies."

So after playing as a semi-professional at Spurs it was no surprise that they let him go. Kerry went off to his home town club of Dunstable, scoring 52 goals in 1979. Reading seeing his considerable potential signed Kerry for £20,000 in the summer of 1980. Their foresight was rewarded as Kerry scored 51 goals in 110 league games at Elm Park, winning the Golden Boot Award for the 1982-83 season.

1904-05 Berks & Bucks Senior League

		P	W	D	L	F	A	Pts
1	Maidenhead North	8	5	2	1	28	12	12
2	**Chesham Generals**	**8**	**5**	**0**	**3**	**19**	**15**	**10**
3	**Chesham Town**	**8**	**4**	**2**	**2**	**15**	**15**	**10**
4	Slough	8	2	3	3	11	14	7
5	Aylesbury	8	0	1	7	7	24	1

1905-06 South Eastern League

		P	W	D	L	F	A	Pts
1	St. Leonards Utd	22	18	1	3	73	18	37
2	Sittingbourne	22	16	4	2	82	26	36
3	Tunbridge Wells Rangers	22	15	3	4	57	19	33
4	Chatham	22	11	6	5	50	34	28
5	Clapton Orient	22	10	3	9	38	36	23
6	Depot Bat RE	22	7	3	12	30	30	17
7	Southern Utd	22	7	3	12	35	57	17
8	West Hampstead	20	7	3	10	24	51	17
9	Tunbridge Wells	22	7	2	13	46	59	16
10	**Chesham Town**	**22**	**6**	**2**	**14**	**28**	**56**	**14**
11	Ashford United	20	5	2	13	30	67	12
12	**Chesham Generals**	**22**	**5**	**0**	**17**	**43**	**83**	**10**

1905-06 Berks & Bucks Senior League

		P	W	D	L	F	A	Pts
1	Reading Reserves	8	6	0	2	30	10	12
2	**Chesham Town**	**8**	**4**	**0**	**4**	**18**	**11**	**8**
3	Aylesbury United	8	4	0	4	16	16	8
4	**Chesham Generals**	**8**	**3**	**0**	**5**	**12**	**24**	**6**
5	Maidenhead United	8	3	0	5	12	27	6

1906-07 South Eastern League

		P	W	D	L	F	A	Pts
1	Southend	18	17	0	1	85	6	34
2	Tunbridge Wells Rangers	18	16	0	2	61	14	32
3	Clapton Orient	18	9	4	5	58	27	22
4	Hastings St. Leonard	18	10	1	7	55	46	21
5	Royal Artillery Btn	18	7	5	6	41	31	19
6	Red Hill	18	4	4	10	33	48	12
7	Eastbourne	18	6	0	12	36	64	12
8	**Chesham Generals**	**18**	**5**	**1**	**12**	**23**	**66**	**11**
9	**Chesham Town**	**18**	**4**	**2**	**12**	**30**	**63**	**10**
10	Tunbridge Wells	18	3	1	14	24	84	7

1907-08 South Eastern League

		P	W	D	L	F	A	Pts
1	Royal Engineers	18	17	0	1	80	7	34
2	Crystal Palace	18	14	3	1	56	13	31
3	**Chesham Town**	**18**	**12**	**2**	**4**	**57**	**35**	**26**
4	Grenadier Guards	18	5	9	4	31	29	19
5	Hastings	18	7	2	9	48	63	16
6	Croydon Common	18	6	3	9	45	53	15
7	**Chesham Generals**	**18**	**5**	**3**	**10**	**42**	**51**	**13**
8	Southend	18	6	1	11	38	64	13
9	Red Hill	18	4	1	13	35	55	9
10	Tunbridge Wells Reserves	18	2	0	16	17	79	4

1908-09 South Eastern League

		P	W	D	L	F	A	Pts
1	**Chesham Town**	**12**	**8**	**0**	**4**	**46**	**18**	**16**
2	Watford Reserves	12	6	3	3	35	19	15
3	Croydon Reserves	12	6	2	4	21	15	14
4	Red Hill	12	7	0	5	28	21	14
5	Metropolitan Gas	12	3	3	6	18	30	9
6	**Chesham Generals**	**12**	**3**	**2**	**7**	**17**	**27**	**8**
7	Leighton Town	12	2	2	8	10	46	6

1909-10 Spartan League

		P	W	D	L	F	A	Pts
1	2nd Coldstream	12	9	1	2	47	12	19
2	Red Hill	12	6	3	3	34	17	15
3	Aylesbury United	12	6	3	3	26	22	15
4	Sutton Court	12	4	3	5	16	26	11
5	Marlow	12	3	4	5	17	34	10
6	Wimbledon	12	2	3	7	15	30	7
7	**Chesham Generals**	**12**	**2**	**3**	**7**	**16**	**32**	**7**

1909-10 South Eastern League

		P	W	D	L	F	A	Pts
1	Peterborough City	10	8	0	2	55	9	16
2	Tunbridge Wells	10	6	2	2	24	15	14
3	**Chesham Town**	**10**	**5**	**3**	**2**	**34**	**15**	**13**
4	**Chesham Generals**	**10**	**4**	**2**	**4**	**20**	**28**	**10**
5	Leighton Town	10	2	3	5	17	38	7
6	Wood Green	10	0	0	10	5	50	0

1911-12 Spartan League

		P	W	D	L	F	A	Pts
1	St Albans	24	21	1	2	71	15	43
2	Coldstream Guards	24	19	3	2	71	19	41
3	Sutton Court	24	13	1	10	56	40	27
4	**Chesham Generals**	**24**	**11**	**4**	**9**	**53**	**41**	**26**
5	Aylesbury United	24	10	5	9	49	44	25
6	3rd Grenadiers	24	10	5	9	37	41	25
7	Cambridge United	24	11	2	11	50	44	24
8	East Ham	24	10	4	10	25	29	24
9	1st Grenadiers	24	9	4	11	48	53	22
10	Polytechnic	24	8	3	13	28	70	19
11	Tufnell Spartans	24	6	4	14	35	53	16
12	Tufnell Park	24	2	8	14	28	51	12
13	Newportians	24	3	2	19	24	73	8

1911-12 Southern League

		P	W	D	L	F	A	Pts
1	Merthyr Town	26	19	3	4	60	14	41
2	Portsmouth	26	19	3	4	73	20	41
3	Cardiff City	26	15	4	7	55	26	34
4	Southend United	26	16	1	9	73	24	33
5	Pontypridd	26	13	6	7	39	24	32
6	Ton Pentre	26	12	3	11	56	45	27
7	Walsall	25	13	1	10	44	41	27
8	Tie Harris	26	11	5	10	44	47	27
9	Aberdare	26	10	3	13	39	44	23
10	Kettering	26	11	0	15	37	62	22
11	Croydon Common	25	8	2	15	43	45	18
12	Mardy	24	6	6	12	37	51	18
13	Cwm Albion	22	5	1	16	27	70	11
14	**Chesham Town**	**26**	**1**	**0**	**25**	**18**	**131**	**2**

Cwm Albion were unable to play four matches because of a coal strike. these remained unplayed.

1912-13 Athenian League

		P	W	D	L	F	A	Pts
1	Catford Southend	16	11	3	2	50	15	25
2	Barnet & Alston	16	9	3	4	36	17	21
3	Tufnell Park	16	8	5	3	25	13	21
4	Finchley	16	8	4	4	19	11	20
5	Grays Athletic	16	4	6	6	18	23	14
6	Chelmsford	16	5	3	8	21	36	13
7	Enfield	16	3	6	7	18	28	12
8	**Chesham Town**	**16**	**3**	**4**	**9**	**21**	**42**	**10**
9	Romford Town	16	2	4	10	17	40	8

1912-13 Spartan League

		P	W	D	L	F	A	Pts
1	2nd Coldstreams	24	20	1	3	73	20	41
2	St Albans City	24	16	4	4	77	24	36
3	**Chesham Generals**	**24**	**16**	**4**	**4**	**60**	**29**	36
4	Newportonians	24	13	3	8	48	37	29
5	Watford Orient	24	11	6	7	72	44	28
6	Aylesbury United	24	11	2	11	40	61	24
7	Cambridge United	24	9	5	10	39	52	23
8	Tufnell Spartans	24	9	3	12	39	47	21
9	Polytechnic	24	6	9	9	26	40	21
10	3rd Grenadiers	24	8	3	13	34	53	19
11	Sutton Court	24	6	5	13	47	59	17
12	East Ham	24	5	1	18	19	57	11
13	Woodford Albion	24	2	2	20	19	76	6

1913-14 Athenian League

		P	W	D	L	F	A	Pts
1	Tufnell Park	22	15	3	4	61	24	33
2	Luton Clarence	22	15	2	5	64	34	32
3	Grays Athletic	22	13	3	6	43	27	29
4	Metrogas	22	11	3	8	62	52	25
5	Enfield	22	10	3	9	52	37	23
6	Barnet & Alston	22	9	4	9	32	28	22
7	Catford Southend	22	7	7	8	35	41	21
8	Romford Town	22	8	5	9	47	65	21
9	Finchley	22	8	3	11	53	47	19
10	Hastings & St Leonards	22	7	2	13	38	59	16
11	Chelmsford	22	6	1	15	32	68	13
12	**Chesham Town**	**22**	**4**	**2**	**16**	**24**	**61**	**10**

1913-14 Spartan League

		P	W	D	L	F	A	Pts
1	**Chesham Generals**	22	17	2	3	47	21	36
2	Aylesbury United	22	16	2	4	60	27	34
3	St Albans City	22	16	3	3	54	16	33
4	2nd Coldstreams	22	11	3	8	30	20	25
5	Newportonians	22	7	6	9	30	41	20
6	Polytechnic	22	7	5	10	30	41	19
7	Gt Western Rly	22	8	3	11	36	56	19
8	Sutton Court	22	7	4	11	41	51	18
9	Tufnell Spartans	22	6	5	11	34	40	17
10	Woodford Albion	22	7	3	12	25	59	17
11	Tunbridge Wells	22	5	6	11	22	41	16
12*	Watford Orient	22	3	2	17	25	58	8

* 2 points deducted

1919-20 Great Western Suburban League

		P	W	D	L	F	A	Pts
1	Maidenhead	22	14	7	1	76	14	35
2	Slough	22	14	4	4	85	37	32
3	Botwell Mission	22	15	2	5	75	32	32
4	Windsor	22	11	5	6	52	33	27
5	Reading United	22	11	2	9	42	40	24
6	Yiewsley	22	10	3	9	49	50	23
7	Wycombe Wanderers	22	7	7	8	57	47	21
8	**Chesham United**	22	8	5	9	42	48	21
9	Marlow	22	7	2	13	40	70	16
10	Newbury	22	5	3	14	34	74	13
11	Uxbridge	22	4	2	16	31	72	10
12	1st Scots Guards	22	4	2	16	29	95	10

1919-20 Spartan League Division I

		P	W	D	L	F	A	Pts
1	Wycombe Wanderers	20	18	1	1	114	24	37
2	GER Romford	20	17	1	2	88	18	35
3	St Albans City	20	13	1	6	64	35	27
4	Aylesbury United	20	12	2	6	49	31	26
5	**Chesham United**	**20**	**11**	**2**	**7**	**58**	**46**	**24**
6	Sutton Court	20	11	2	7	54	45	24
7	Polytechnic	19	6	0	13	42	65	12
8	Tufnell Spartans	20	5	1	14	41	70	11
9	Newportians	20	4	3	13	25	67	11
10	Great Western Railway	20	3	0	17	20	79	6
11	2nd Coldstream Guards	19	2	1	16	19	93	5

1920-21 Spartan League Division I

		P	W	D	L	F	A	Pts
1	Wycombe Wanderers	22	19	2	1	108	29	40
2	Slough	22	16	4	2	74	20	36
3	**Chesham United**	**22**	**16**	**3**	**3**	**88**	**34**	**36**
4	Great Eastern Railway	22	15	1	6	87	36	31
5	Leavesdon Mental Hospital	22	13	4	5	42	29	30
6	Wood Green	22	9	5	8	55	54	23
7	Aylesbury United	22	10	1	11	44	52	21
8	Sutton Court	22	6	4	12	47	71	16
9	Polytechnic	22	5	5	12	37	53	15
10	Great Western Railway	22	2	2	18	34	100	6
11	1st Welsh Guards	22	1	4	17	24	79	6
12	Newportians	22	0	5	17	18	79	5

1920-21 Spartan League Division II

		P	W	D	L	F	A	Pts
1	Wycombe Wanderers	14	10	3	1	61	18	23
2	Cubitts (Aylesbury)	14	9	2	3	37	29	20
3	**Chesham United**	**14**	**6**	**2**	**6**	**44**	**30**	**14**
4	Aylesbury United	14	6	2	6	32	35	14
5	Polytechnic	14	7	0	7	28	34	14
6	RAF Uxbridge	14	4	1	9	31	41	9
7	Slough	14	4	1	9	26	43	9
8	Great Eastern Railway	14	3	3	8	21	39	9

1921-22 Spartan League Division I

		P	W	D	L	F	A	Pts
1	**Chesham United**	**26**	**19**	**2**	**5**	**113**	**29**	**40**
2	Slough	26	18	4	4	101	40	40
3	Finchley	26	15	4	7	67	36	34
4	Aylesbury United	26	15	3	8	71	54	33
5	Leavesdon M H	26	11	11	4	44	31	33
6	Wood Green	26	12	5	9	54	44	29
7	Gt Eastern Railway	26	13	2	11	68	49	28
8	Walthamstow Avenue	26	13	2	11	55	46	28
9	Polytechnic	26	10	6	10	53	49	26
10	Hertford Town	26	10	5	11	58	65	25
11	Sutton Court	26	9	3	14	59	70	21
12	Leyland Motors	26	5	3	18	24	76	13
13	Railway Clearing House	26	4	4	18	26	105	12
14	1st Welsh Guards	26	1	0	25	22	121	2

1921-22 Spartan League Division II

		P	W	D	L	F	A	Pts
1	**Chesham United Res**	**18**	**14**	**1**	**3**	**71**	**23**	**29**
2	Aylesbury United Res	18	12	3	3	47	25	27
3	Finchley Res	18	10	5	3	56	28	25
4	Cubitts (Aylesbury)	18	11	2	5	75	26	24
5	Gt Eastern Railway Res	18	8	3	7	43	42	19
6	Slough Res	18	8	1	9	40	49	17
7	Walthamstow Avenue	18	7	2	9	40	40	16
8	Polytechnic Res	18	4	2	12	24	56	10
9	Gt Western Railway	18	4	1	13	20	57	9
10	Leyland Motor Res	18	1	2	15	25	95	4

1922-23 Spartan League Division I

		P	W	D	L	F	A	Pts
1	**Chesham United**	**26**	**20**	**3**	**3**	**106**	**29**	**43**
2	Wealdstone	26	16	3	7	72	44	35
3	Slough	26	15	2	9	68	55	32
4	Maidenhead	26	12	8	6	47	51	32
5	Leavesdon M H	26	13	3	10	50	40	29
6	Gt Eastern Railway	26	13	3	10	53	50	29
7	Walthamstow Avenue	26	11	6	9	58	51	28
8	Wood Green	26	11	2	13	46	48	24
9	Hertford Town	26	9	5	12	55	50	23
10	Aylesbury United	26	10	2	14	47	60	22
11	Old Latymerians	26	10	0	16	65	80	20
12	Polytechnic	26	8	4	14	35	59	20
13	Finchley	26	6	3	17	36	59	15
14	Old Lyonians	26	3	6	17	38	83	12

1923-24 Spartan League Division I

		P	W	D	L	F	A	Pts
1	Leavesdon M H	26	21	1	4	66	46	43
2	Gt Eastern Railway	26	18	3	5	77	29	39
3	Slough	26	18	2	6	90	33	38
4	Aylesbury United	26	15	4	7	70	36	34
5	Wealdstone	26	14	5	7	71	47	33
6	**Chesham United**	**26**	**14**	**1**	**11**	**68**	**59**	**29**
7	Wood Green	26	10	3	13	67	62	23
8	Hertford Town	26	11	1	14	61	77	23
9	Polytechnic	26	11	1	14	42	57	23
10	Walthamstow Avenue	26	11	8	10	52	65	22
11	Old Lyonians	26	7	4	15	39	68	18
12	Maidenhead	26	7	3	16	44	47	17
13	RAF Uxbridge	26	5	3	18	39	95	13
14	Old Latymerians	26	3	1	22	33	100	7

1924-25 Spartan League Division I

		P	W	D	L	F	A	Pts
1	**Chesham United**	26	21	4	1	107	32	46
2	Gt Eastern Rly, Romford	26	17	4	5	74	37	38
3	Slough	26	17	1	8	90	54	35
4	Botwell Mission	26	13	3	10	69	42	29
5	Staines Town	26	12	5	9	57	51	29
6	Walthamstow Avenue	26	11	5	10	59	66	27
7	RAF Uxbridge	26	11	5	10	56	73	27
8	Hertford Town	26	11	4	11	56	52	26
9	Maidenhead United	26	9	2	15	55	66	20
10	Wealdstone	26	7	6	13	48	62	20
11	Wood Green	26	8	4	14	53	73	20
12	Aylesbury United	26	8	3	15	51	79	19
13	Sutton Court	26	6	3	17	37	81	15
14	Polytechnic	26	5	3	18	38	84	13

1925-26 Spartan League Division I

		P	W	D	L	F	A	Pts
1	Gt Eastern Rly, Romford	28	21	3	4	97	47	45
2	Botwell Mission	28	20	3	5	109	51	43
3	Maidenhead United	28	19	3	6	122	64	41
4	Walthamstow Avenue	28	17	5	6	103	61	39
5	**Chesham United**	28	15	6	7	100	59	36
6	Slough	28	17	2	9	81	50	36
7	Wealdstone	28	13	4	11	79	80	30
8	Aylesbury United	28	13	2	13	78	86	28
9	Wood Green	28	9	7	12	62	83	25
10	Colchester	28	10	4	14	63	94	24
11	Staines Town	28	6	6	16	75	90	18
12	Polytechnic	28	6	5	17	60	98	17
13	Hertford Town	28	7	3	18	73	120	17
14	Sutton Court	28	5	2	21	59	111	12

1926-27 Spartan League Division I

		P	W	D	L	F	A	Pts
1	Maidenhead	28	19	5	4	116	51	43
2	**Chesham United**	28	18	4	6	83	41	40
3	Slough	28	18	4	6	96	53	40
4	Wealdstone	28	18	3	7	100	67	39
5	Gt Eastern Rly, Romford	28	16	4	8	85	68	36
6	Walthamstow Avenue	28	15	5	8	96	60	35
7	Botwell Mission	28	14	2	12	71	57	30
8	Aylesbury United	28	12	5	11	77	85	29
9	Lyons	28	10	8	10	64	55	28
10	Staines Town	28	10	6	12	85	94	26
11	Colchester	28	10	4	14	64	74	24
12	Wood Green	28	6	3	19	57	92	15
13	Hertford Town	28	6	3	19	61	118	15
14	Polytechnic	28	4	6	18	54	102	14

1927-28 Spartan League Division I

		P	W	D	L	F	A	Pts
1	Botwell Mission	28	22	2	4	106	46	46
2	Walthamstow Avenue	28	21	2	5	106	48	44
3	**Chesham United**	28	18	5	5	101	44	41
4	Wealdstone	28	17	3	8	90	62	37
5	Maidenhead United	28	15	4	9	103	57	34
6	Gt Eastern Rly, Romford	28	11	8	9	74	67	30
7	Staines Town	28	12	6	10	65	76	30
8	Aylesbury United	28	13	2	13	89	69	28
9	Slough	28	12	4	12	82	73	28
10	Lyons Club	28	11	6	11	47	58	28
11	Colchester Town	28	10	5	13	69	74	25
12	Berkhamsted Town	28	10	1	17	52	83	21
13	Hertford Town	28	7	4	17	51	114	18
14	Polytechnic	28	2	2	24	33	100	6
15	Wood Green	28	2	0	26	46	143	4

1928-29 Spartan League Division I

		P	W	D	L	F	A	Pts
1	Aylesbury United	24	19	1	4	113	47	38
2	Maidenhead United	24	17	3	4	91	45	37
3	Botwell Mission	24	14	4	6	87	64	32
4	**Chesham United**	**24**	**14**	**1**	**9**	**78**	**50**	**29**
5	Staines Town	24	11	5	8	73	52	27
6	Egham	24	10	7	7	45	49	27
7	Leighton Town	24	11	2	11	59	66	24
8	Slough	24	10	2	12	54	65	22
9	Cowley Oxford	24	6	7	11	47	59	19
10	Leagrave & District	24	7	4	13	45	65	18
11	Berkhamsted Town	24	5	7	12	42	64	17
12	Watford Old Boys	24	5	3	16	48	91	13
13	RAF Uxbridge	24	3	3	18	32	87	9

1929-30 Spartan League Premier Division

		P	W	D	L	F	A	Pts
1	Met Police	26	19	4	3	98	26	42
2	**Chesham United**	**26**	**19**	**2**	**5**	**85**	**51**	**40**
3	Hayes	26	15	6	5	92	53	36
4	Egham	26	16	2	8	58	27	34
5	Maidenhead United	26	14	3	9	85	56	31
6	Brentwood & Warley	26	12	5	9	61	50	29
7	Crittalls Athletic	26	12	4	10	62	44	28
8	Slough	26	10	4	12	57	63	24
9	Colchester Town	26	9	6	11	53	71	24
10	Aylesbury United	26	8	3	15	64	96	19
11	Lyons Club	26	7	5	14	35	70	19
12	G E, Romford	26	6	2	18	43	83	14
13	Wood Green	26	4	5	17	39	90	13
14	Staines Town	26	3	5	18	35	87	9

1930-31 Spartan League Premier Division

		P	W	D	L	F	A	Pts
1	Haywards	26	21	2	3	130	48	44
2	Maidenhead United	26	18	5	3	94	39	41
3	Met Police	26	18	2	6	78	39	38
4	**Chesham United**	**26**	**16**	**2**	**8**	**81**	**53**	**34**
5	Slough	26	14	2	10	73	53	30
6+	Hounslow	26	11	4	11	59	59	28
7	Brentwood & Warley	26	11	3	12	56	57	25
8*	Crittals Athletic	26	10	6	10	54	67	24
9	Colchester Town	26	10	0	16	72	81	20
10*	Aylesbury United	26	10	1	15	71	98	19
11	Egham	26	8	2	16	42	67	18
12	Lyons Club	26	8	1	17	55	88	17
13	Wood Green	26	8	1	17	47	87	17
14	G E, Romford	26	3	1	22	41	117	7

+ 2 points added *2 points deducted*

1931-32 Spartan League Premier Division

		P	W	D	L	F	A	Pts
1	Maidenhead United	24	18	3	3	76	37	39
2	Slough	24	13	7	4	68	46	33
3	**Chesham United**	**24**	**14**	**4**	**6**	**64**	**41**	**32**
4	Hitchin	24	13	3	8	56	46	29
5	Colchester Town	24	12	3	9	71	63	27
6	Met Police	24	11	4	9	57	40	26
7	Aylesbury United	24	11	4	9	64	50	26
8	Hounslow	24	11	1	12	48	54	23
9	Windsor	24	8	2	14	57	66	18
10	Brentwood & Warley	24	7	4	13	49	66	18
11	Crittalls Athletic	24	7	3	14	44	72	17
12	Lyons Club	24	6	4	14	36	65	16
13	Egham	24	3	2	19	39	83	8

1932-33 Spartan League Premier Division

		P	W	D	L	F	A	Pts
1	**Chesham United**	26	18	1	7	78	39	37
2	Slough	26	17	0	9	81	58	34
3	Callender Athletic	26	14	5	7	62	46	33
4	Crittall Athletic	26	14	3	9	55	48	31
5	Colchester Town	26	14	3	9	78	75	31
6	Met Police	26	15	0	11	56	42	30
7	Brentwood & Warley	26	13	2	11	61	61	28
8	Hitchin Town	26	11	5	10	74	57	27
9	Maidenhead United	26	11	4	11	68	64	26
10	Wood Green Town	26	9	3	14	47	67	21
11	Hounslow Town	26	9	3	14	46	70	21
12	Windsor & Eton	26	8	1	17	46	75	17
13	Apsley	26	5	4	17	50	77	14
14	Aylesbury United	26	6	2	18	41	73	14

1933-34 Spartan League Premier Division

		P	W	D	L	F	A	Pts
1	Maidenhead United	26	19	6	1	84	40	44
2	**Chesham United**	26	17	3	6	68	88	37
3	Met Police	26	15	2	9	79	59	32
4	Waterlow's (Dunstable)	26	13	3	10	72	54	29
5	Hitchin Town	26	12	4	10	52	46	28
6	Letchworth Town	26	11	5	10	49	49	27
7	Windsor & Eton	26	11	5	10	49	66	27
8	Colchester Town	26	11	4	11	70	66	26
9	Crittall Athletic	26	10	5	11	56	59	25
10	Callender Athletic	26	11	1	14	50	53	23
11	Slough	26	9	3	14	57	64	21
12	Hounslow Town	26	8	3	15	48	69	19
13	Brentwood & Warley	26	5	4	17	34	68	14
14	Wood Green Town	26	5	2	19	34	71	12

1934-35 Spartan League Premier Division

		P	W	D	L	F	A	Pts
1	Hitchin Town	26	18	2	6	65	33	38
2	Met Police	26	17	4	5	53	28	38
3	Hoxton	26	13	3	10	61	41	29
4	Slough	26	13	3	10	67	50	29
5	Waterlow's (Dunstable)	26	13	2	11	85	67	28
6	Maidenhead United	26	10	7	9	63	61	27
7	Colchester Town	26	12	2	12	60	76	26
8	Callender Athletic	26	8	8	10	42	42	24
9	**Chesham United**	**26**	**9**	**6**	**11**	**57**	**64**	**24**
10	Windsor & Eton	26	10	2	14	47	54	22
11	Crittall Athletic	26	8	6	12	48	59	22
12	Letchworth Town	26	10	2	14	45	69	22
13	Apsley	26	10	1	15	57	65	21
14	Hounslow Town	26	5	2	18	39	80	12

1935-36 Spartan League Premier Division

		P	W	D	L	F	A	Pts
1	Waterlow's (Dunstable)	26	19	2	5	107	55	40
2	Callender Athletic	26	18	2	6	90	61	38
3	**Chesham United**	**26**	**14**	**4**	**8**	**59**	**57**	**32**
4	Cambridge Town	26	13	4	9	67	58	30
5	Met Police	26	13	2	11	57	52	28
6	Hitchin Town	26	10	5	11	60	59	25
7	Maidenhead United	26	10	5	11	67	72	25
8	Windsor & Eton	26	11	2	13	63	55	24
9	Slough	26	11	2	13	53	67	24
10	Hoxton Manor	26	10	3	13	49	50	23
11	Jurgens (Purfleet)	26	11	1	14	54	66	23
12	Aylesbury United	26	8	5	13	51	77	21
13	Apsley	26	8	2	16	68	83	18
14	Letchworth Town	26	7	18	1	59	97	15

1936-37 Spartan League Premier Division

		P	W	D	L	F	A	Pts
1	Met Police	26	16	4	6	90	47	36
2	Windsor & Eton	26	16	3	7	81	60	35
3	Waterlow's (Dunstable)	26	16	2	8	99	65	34
4	Hitchin Town	26	14	4	8	66	44	32
5	Callender Athletic	26	15	2	9	71	58	32
6	Cambridge Town	26	11	8	7	59	49	30
7	Hoxton Manor	26	11	3	12	56	54	25
8	**Chesham United**	**26**	**10**	**4**	**12**	**55**	**68**	**24**
9	Maidenhead United	26	10	2	14	67	67	22
10	Aylesbury United	26	9	4	13	57	81	22
11	Lyons Club	26	9	3	14	57	77	21
12	Slough	26	8	3	15	62	73	19
13	Hoddesdon Town	26	6	5	15	51	82	17
14	Jurgens (Purfleet)	26	7	1	18	44	90	15

1937-38 Spartan League Premier Division

		P	W	D	L	F	A	Pts
1	Waterlows (Dunstable)	26	18	4	4	95	53	40
2	Windsor and Eton	26	17	3	6	67	42	37
3	Callender Athletic	26	15	5	6	62	41	35
4	**Chesham United**	**26**	**14**	**6**	**6**	**74**	**30**	**34**
5	Hitchin Town	26	14	4	8	71	36	32
6	Slough	26	14	3	9	77	61	31
7	Met Police	26	15	1	10	67	47	31
8	Cambridge Town	26	11	4	11	52	65	26
9	Maidenhead Town	26	8	7	11	46	55	23
10	Hoxton Manor	26	8	4	14	46	63	20
11	Lyons Club	26	6	7	13	36	62	19
12	Letchworth Town	26	8	2	16	46	83	18
13	Aylesbury United	26	4	4	18	44	81	12
14	Henley Town	26	1	4	21	39	124	6

1938-39 Spartan League Premier Division

		P	W	D	L	F	A	Pts
1	Met Police	26	17	6	3	92	33	40
2	Slough	26	15	6	5	72	43	36
3	Hitchin Town	26	15	5	6	93	39	35
4	Waterlows (Dunstable)	26	13	7	6	71	47	33
5	Cambridge Town	26	12	8	6	49	39	32
6	**Chesham United**	**26**	**12**	**5**	**9**	**60**	**59**	**29**
7	Windsor and Eton	26	12	3	11	84	56	27
8	Wood Green Town	26	11	5	10	56	68	27
9	Maidenhead Town	26	7	8	11	49	70	22
10	Callender Athletic	26	7	6	13	46	63	20
11	Lyons Club	26	7	5	14	39	83	17
12	Marlow	26	7	3	16	52	83	17
13	Hoxton Manor	26	4	6	16	32	63	14
14	Letchworth Town	26	6	1	19	34	81	13

1939-40 Great Western Combination

		P	W	D	L	F	A	Pts
1	Hayes	18	15	1	2	60	20	31
2	Wycombe Wanderers	18	11	1	6	58	49	23
3	Slough	18	8	5	5	43	37	21
4	Wycombe Redfords	18	7	5	5	41	33	19
5	**Chesham United**	**18**	**9**	**1**	**8**	**53**	**43**	**19**
6	Maidenhead United	18	7	4	7	40	36	18
7	Uxbridge Town	18	6	2	10	35	47	14
8	Henley Town	18	6	2	10	47	62	14
9	Marlow	*17	3	5	9	25	42	11
10	Windsor & Eton	*17	3	2	12	32	85	8

* One game not played

1940-41 Great Western Combination

		P	W	D	L	F	A	Pts
1	Oxford City	18	13	3	2	70	30	29
2	Reading Reserves	18	12	3	3	57	40	27
3	Windsor & Eton	18	12	2	4	64	30	26
4	**Chesham United**	**18**	**10**	**1**	**7**	**51**	**44**	**21**
5	Wycombe Wanderers	18	10	1	7	47	41	21
6	Marlow	18	8	3	7	46	40	19
7	Uxbridge Town	18	5	2	11	41	43	12
8	Maidenhead United	18	4	1	13	37	74	9
9	High Duty Alloys	18	2	4	12	41	88	8
10	Wycombe Redfords	18	1	6	11	21	47	8

1941-42 Great Western Combination

		P	W	D	L	F	A	Pts
1	Oxford City	18	15	3	0	78	30	33
2	Grenadier Guards	18	11	2	5	56	37	24
3	Wycombe Wanderers	18	12	0	6	62	44	24
4	Windsor & Eton	18	12	0	6	72	57	24
5	**Chesham United**	**18**	**7**	**4**	**7**	**35**	**44**	**18**
6	Marlow	18	7	1	10	45	52	15
7	Reading Reserves	18	7	1	10	53	65	15
8	Uxbridge Town	18	4	3	11	41	46	11
9	Maidenhead United	18	3	4	11	42	63	10
10	High Duty Alloys	18	2	2	14	26	72	6

1945-46 Spartan League Western Division

		P	W	D	L	F	A	Pts
1	Hounslow	18	12	1	5	61	23	25
2	Aylesbury	18	11	1	6	70	47	23
3	**Chesham United**	**18**	**9**	**4**	**5**	**55**	**29**	**22**
4	Marlow	18	9	2	7	60	64	20
5	Leighton United	18	10	0	8	47	62	20
6	Polytechnic	18	7	5	6	44	37	19
7	Yiewsley	18	7	4	7	51	46	18
8	Berkhamsted	18	6	2	10	42	54	14
9	Henley	18	5	2	11	55	71	12
10	Apsley	18	2	3	13	32	74	7

1946-47 Spartan League Premier Division

		P	W	D	L	F	A	Pts
1	Met Police	26	21	2	3	100	29	44
2	Vauxhall	26	20	2	4	112	50	42
3	Letchworth	26	16	5	5	74	54	37
4	Hoddesden	26	15	4	7	96	73	34
5	Cambridge Town	26	13	3	10	95	40	29
6	Wood Green	26	12	5	9	79	65	29
7	Harrow	26	13	2	11	62	55	28
8	**Chesham United**	**26**	**12**	**2**	**12**	**74**	**74**	**26**
9	Bishops Stortford	26	7	5	14	57	69	19
10	Aylesbury	26	8	3	15	51	78	19
11	Pinner	26	6	5	15	43	72	17
12	Lyons Club	26	8	1	17	51	106	17
13	Crown & Anchor	26	7	2	17	41	94	16
14	Hertford	26	3	1	22	34	110	7

1947-48 Corinthian Football League

		P	W	D	L	F	A	Pts
1	Walton & Hersham	26	17	4	5	82	40	38
2	Hounslow	26	16	2	8	68	46	34
3	Erith & Belvedere	26	15	3	8	67	38	33
4	Carshalton Athletic	26	15	2	9	70	53	32
5	Grays Athletic	26	13	5	8	68	56	31
6	Edgware Town	26	12	5	9	55	46	29
7	Hastings & St Leonards	26	12	3	11	72	57	27
8	Maidenhead United	26	10	5	11	45	52	25
9	Eastbourne	26	10	4	12	55	68	24
10	Uxbridge	26	10	3	13	53	62	23
11	**Chesham United**	**26**	**6**	**9**	**11**	**48**	**60**	**21**
12	Windsor & Eton	26	9	3	14	42	75	21
13	Slough Town	26	7	4	15	50	51	18
14	Bedford Avenue	26	4	0	22	35	106	8

1948-49 Corinthian Football League

		P	W	D	L	F	A	Pts
1	Walton & Hersham	24	19	1	4	82	32	39
2	Uxbridge	24	14	5	5	52	36	33
3	Hounslow Town	24	13	6	5	67	45	32
4	Erith & Belvedere	24	13	5	6	54	39	31
5	Grays Athletic	24	12	4	8	73	58	28
6	Slough Town	24	10	6	8	55	38	26
7	Worthing	24	7	7	10	49	60	21
8	**Chesham United**	**24**	**8**	**5**	**11**	**42**	**75**	**21**
9	Maidenhead United	24	8	4	12	34	48	20
10	Carshalton Athletic	24	7	3	14	48	59	17
11	Edgware Town	24	4	8	12	35	43	16
12	Eastbourne	24	6	4	14	49	68	16
13	Windsor & Eton	24	6	0	18	35	74	12

Hastings & St Leonards withdrew after one match, which has been excluded from the results.

1949-50 Corinthian Football League

		P	W	D	L	F	A	Pts
1	Hounslow Town	26	19	3	4	86	37	41
2	Walton & Hersham	26	18	4	4	69	31	40
3	Erith & Belvedere	26	14	6	6	59	30	34
4	Uxbridge	26	15	3	8	65	47	33
5	Worthing	26	12	4	10	57	50	28
6	Grays Athletic	26	10	8	8	63	62	28
7	Eastbourne	26	10	7	9	52	46	27
8	Slough Town	26	10	7	9	46	51	27
9	Edgware Town	26	10	5	11	50	53	25
10	Maidenhead United	26	7	8	11	43	46	22
11	**Chesham United**	**26**	**7**	**8**	**11**	**53**	**59**	**22**
12	Carshalton Athletic	26	8	4	14	56	75	20
13	Epsom	26	2	5	19	38	95	9
14	Windsor & Eton	26	3	2	21	34	89	8

1950-51 Corinthian Football League

		P	W	D	L	F	A	Pts
1	Slough Town	26	17	4	5	65	33	38
2	Hounslow Town	26	17	3	6	80	41	37
3	Erith & Belvedere	26	13	5	8	59	43	31
4	Edgware Town	26	14	2	10	65	52	30
5	Maidenhead United	26	13	3	10	57	49	29
6	Grays Athletic	26	11	5	10	68	54	27
7	**Chesham United**	**26**	**11**	**4**	**11**	**69**	**61**	**26**
8	Tilbury	26	11	4	11	42	44	26
9	Uxbridge	26	10	4	12	64	62	24
10	Worthing	26	11	2	13	52	75	24
11	Carshalton Athletic	26	8	4	14	65	75	20
12	Eastbourne	26	8	3	15	47	65	19
13	Epsom	26	8	2	16	61	94	18
14	Maidstone United	26	6	3	17	58	104	15

1951-52 Corinthian Football League

		P	W	D	L	F	A	Pts
1	Hounslow Town	26	21	1	4	84	28	43
2	Grays Athletic	26	19	5	2	77	35	43
3	Slough Town	26	19	3	4	85	37	41
4	Erith & Belvedere	26	14	1	11	56	50	29
5	Carshalton Athletic	26	10	7	9	67	59	27
6	**Chesham United**	**26**	**12**	**2**	**12**	**64**	**62**	**26**
7	Tilbury	26	11	4	11	46	58	26
8	Eastbourne	26	9	7	10	53	53	25
9	Epsom	26	9	4	13	45	65	22
10	Worthing	26	8	6	12	44	68	22
11	Uxbridge	26	8	5	13	59	58	21
12	Edgware Town	26	5	5	16	37	60	15
13	Maidstone United	26	3	7	16	40	80	13
14	Maidenhead United	26	5	1	20	28	72	11

1952-53 Corinthian Football League

		P	W	D	L	F	A	Pts
1	Carshalton Athletic	26	19	1	6	70	44	39
2	Hounslow Town	26	16	4	6	84	46	36
3	Epsom	26	16	2	8	72	39	34
4	Maidstone United	26	14	4	8	58	53	32
5	Uxbridge	26	12	5	9	40	41	29
6	Grays Athletic	26	11	6	9	58	47	28
7	Edgware Town	26	11	6	9	65	54	28
8	Tilbury	26	10	5	11	46	42	25
9	Maidenhead United	26	9	5	12	44	50	23
10	Slough Town	26	7	7	12	39	53	21
11	Eastbourne	26	7	7	12	40	58	21
12	Erith & Belvedere	26	8	4	14	43	50	20
13	**Chesham United**	**26**	**5**	**4**	**17**	**33**	**64**	**14**
14	Worthing	26	6	2	18	29	80	14

1953-54 Corinthian Football League

		P	W	D	L	F	A	Pts
1	Carshalton Athletic	26	17	5	4	75	41	39
2	Edgware Town	26	17	4	5	75	41	38
3	Hounslow Town	26	13	8	5	75	45	34
4	Maidstone United	26	13	7	6	60	43	33
5	Grays Athletic	26	12	2	12	62	50	26
6	Tilbury	26	10	6	10	60	56	26
7	Erith & Belvedere	26	10	6	10	45	55	26
8	Eastbourne	26	10	5	11	47	45	25
9	Uxbridge	26	11	3	12	45	56	25
10	Epsom	26	11	1	14	54	64	23
11	Worthing	26	7	6	13	52	66	20
12	Maidenhead United	26	7	4	15	46	71	18
13	Slough Town	26	5	7	14	49	60	17
14	**Chesham United**	**26**	**4**	**4**	**18**	**38**	**90**	**12**

1954-55 Corinthian Football League

		P	W	D	L	F	A	Pts
1	Hounslow Town	28	22	3	3	80	37	47
2	Grays Athletic	28	18	3	7	74	41	39
3	Carshalton Athletic	28	17	4	7	65	38	38
4	Slough Town	28	12	10	6	58	49	34
5	Uxbridge	28	11	8	9	62	46	30
6	Maidenhead United	28	11	6	11	50	63	28
7	Yiewsley	28	12	3	13	49	46	27
8	Edgware Town	28	10	7	11	58	60	27
9	**Chesham United**	**28**	**12**	**3**	**13**	**56**	**73**	**27**
10	Erith & Belvedere	28	10	8	10	57	56	26
11	Worthing	28	10	4	14	54	62	24
12	Maidstone United	28	9	5	14	48	50	23
13	Tilbury	28	9	5	14	47	56	23
14	Eastbourne	28	3	7	18	24	63	13
15	Epsom	28	3	6	19	41	83	12

Erith & Belvedere had two points deducted.

1955-56 Corinthian Football League

		P	W	D	L	F	A	Pts
1	Maidstone United	26	19	3	4	74	37	41
2	Yiewsley	26	15	5	6	62	31	35
3	Uxbridge	26	14	5	7	56	34	33
4	Slough Town	26	14	5	7	59	38	33
5	Epsom	26	14	3	9	58	42	31
6	Grays Athletic	26	13	3	10	48	48	29
7	Maidenhead United	26	12	4	10	56	47	28
8	Carshalton Athletic	26	12	3	11	50	41	27
9	Tilbury	26	9	6	11	43	55	24
10	Edgware Town	26	7	7	12	30	49	21
11	Worthing	26	7	5	14	57	71	19
12	Eastbourne	26	6	4	16	29	54	16
13	Erith & Belvedere	26	6	2	18	32	69	14
14	**Chesham United**	**26**	**6**	**1**	**19**	**36**	**74**	**13**

1955-56 Reserve Section

		P	W	D	L	F	A	Pts
1	Carshalton Athletic	26	18	5	3	107	31	41
2	Greys Athletic	26	18	4	4	86	43	40
3	Yiewsley	26	15	6	5	71	31	36
4	**Chesham United**	**26**	**15**	**2**	**8**	**55**	**49**	**32**
5	Epsom	26	14	3	9	67	51	31
6	Tilbury	26	11	5	9	45	47	27
7	Maidstone United	26	12	2	12	75	67	26
8	Edgware Town	26	8	7	11	48	71	23
9	Slough Town	26	9	4	13	79	77	22
10	Eastbourne	26	9	4	13	43	54	22
11	Maidenhead United	26	7	6	13	61	74	20
12	Uxbridge	26	5	6	15	39	75	16
13	Worthing	26	5	4	17	34	83	14
14	Erith & Belvedere	26	3	6	17	34	91	12

1956-57 Corinthian Football League

		P	W	D	L	F	A	Pts
1	Yiewsley	28	18	6	4	73	35	42
2	Grays Athletic	28	16	8	4	81	43	40
3	Maidenhead United	28	15	6	7	88	50	39
4	Epsom	28	18	2	8	76	37	38
5	Maidstone United	28	15	6	7	80	40	36
6	Slough Town	28	12	9	7	63	42	33
7	Eastbourne	28	12	6	10	67	56	30
8	Uxbridge	28	12	6	10	54	52	30
9	Wembley	28	9	8	11	53	55	26
10	Erith & Belvedere	28	11	3	14	51	66	25
11	Edgware Town	28	8	5	15	48	72	21
12	Dorking	28	7	5	16	51	80	19
13	Tilbury	28	8	3	17	31	78	19
14	**Chesham United**	**28**	**4**	**5**	**19**	**38**	**83**	**13**
15	Worthing	28	2	5	21	34	99	9

1956-57 Reserve Section

		P	W	D	L	F	A	Pts
1	Yiewsley	28	20	4	4	96	41	44
2	Maidenhead United	28	17	6	5	114	57	40
3	Grays Athletic	28	17	3	8	75	45	37
4	Wembley	28	16	4	8	57	39	36
5	Maidstone United	28	13	6	9	75	59	32
6	Slough Town	28	14	3	11	71	71	31
7	Uxbridge	28	13	3	12	66	59	29
8	Eastbourne	28	14	0	14	62	52	28
9	Dorking	28	11	6	11	66	75	28
10	Erith & Belvedere	28	9	6	13	54	67	24
11	Edgware Town	28	10	4	14	49	66	24
12	Epsom	28	6	6	16	48	73	18
13	Tilbury	28	7	4	17	48	95	18
14	**Chesham United**	**28**	**4**	**9**	**15**	**43**	**81**	**17**
15	Worthing	28	4	6	18	44	88	14

1957-58 Corinthian Football League

		P	W	D	L	F	A	Pts
1	Maidenhead United	28	20	3	5	65	39	43
2	Slough Town	28	18	6	4	72	41	42
3	Grays Athletic	28	17	6	5	82	28	40
4	Yiewsley	28	13	8	7	56	36	34
5	Edgware Town	28	13	5	10	59	54	31
6	Uxbridge	28	12	7	9	57	53	31
7	Dagenham	28	11	8	9	38	40	30
8	Epsom	28	12	5	11	64	60	29
9	Erith & Belvedere	28	11	2	15	44	57	24
10	Eastbourne	28	7	9	12	40	50	23
11	Wembley	28	9	4	15	48	54	22
12	**Chesham United**	**28**	**9**	**4**	**15**	**40**	**50**	**22**
13	Horsham	28	6	5	17	50	77	17
14	Dorking	28	4	9	15	37	63	17
15	Worthing	28	6	3	19	48	98	15

1958-59 Corinthian Football League

		P	W	D	L	F	A	Pts
1	Dagenham	26	19	2	5	70	36	40
2	Maidenhead United	26	14	7	5	63	38	35
3	Slough Town	26	14	5	7	75	41	33
4	Wembley	26	13	4	9	61	44	30
5	Leatherhead	26	13	4	9	58	54	30
6	Dorking	26	9	8	9	45	40	26
7	Uxbridge	26	11	3	12	58	63	25
8	Edgware Town	26	11	3	12	49	67	25
9	Horsham	26	9	5	12	66	68	23
10	Erith & Belvedere	26	8	7	11	43	53	23
11	**Chesham United**	**26**	**8**	**6**	**12**	**45**	**57**	**22**
12	Epsom	26	8	6	12	44	57	22
13	Eastbourne	26	5	7	14	28	50	17
14	Worthing	26	5	3	18	45	82	13

1959-60 Corinthian Football League

		P	W	D	L	F	A	Pts
1	Uxbridge	30	20	4	6	72	40	44
2	Maidenhead United	30	16	6	8	70	40	38
3	Dorking	30	17	3	10	69	47	37
4	Epsom	30	17	2	11	70	55	36
5	Letchworth Town	30	14	6	10	68	62	34
6	Dagenham	30	13	7	10	50	40	33
7	Slough Town	30	14	4	12	54	53	32
8	Horsham	30	13	5	12	68	64	31
9	Wokingham Town	30	11	7	12	62	51	29
10	Worthing	30	11	7	12	70	74	29
11	Erith & Belvedere	30	10	9	11	62	66	29
12	Leatherhead	30	12	3	15	56	63	27
13	**Chesham United**	**30**	**11**	**4**	**15**	**45**	**60**	**26**
14	Wembley	30	11	3	16	56	77	25
15	Eastbourne	30	8	4	18	41	67	20
16	Edgware Town	30	4	2	24	37	91	10

1960-61 Corinthian Football League

		P	W	D	L	F	A	Pts
1	Maidenhead United	30	19	5	6	65	39	43
2	**Chesham United**	**30**	**19**	**2**	**9**	**73**	**38**	**40**
3	Edgware Town	30	17	6	7	70	40	40
4	Dagenham	30	18	3	9	82	55	39
5	Horsham	30	17	3	10	85	77	37
6	Uxbridge	30	15	5	10	50	40	35
7	Worthing	30	14	5	11	85	67	33
8	Letchworth	30	15	3	12	64	66	33
9	Dorking	30	12	6	12	64	61	30
10	Erith & Belvedere	30	10	7	13	59	57	27
11	Eastbourne	30	10	6	14	50	59	26
12	Epsom & Ewell	30	11	3	16	46	77	25
13	Leatherhead	30	9	4	17	68	93	22
14	Wokingham	30	8	5	17	44	60	21
15	Wembley	30	6	6	18	51	80	18
16	Slough Town	30	4	3	23	48	95	11

1960-61 Corinthian Football League Reserves

		P	W	D	L	F	A	Pts
1	Wokingham	30	22	6	2	97	32	50
2	Edgware Town	30	19	6	5	88	38	44
3	Maidenhead United	30	19	6	5	82	51	44
4	Dagenham	30	18	7	5	95	30	43
5	**Chesham United**	**30**	**20**	**3**	**7**	**78**	**51**	**43**
6	Horsham	30	17	4	9	85	61	38
7	Uxbridge	30	13	6	11	67	61	32
8	Erith & Belvedere	29	9	9	11	62	69	27
9	Letchworth	30	11	2	17	59	72	24
10	Epsom & Ewell	29	8	7	14	56	73	23
11	Leatherhead	30	6	8	16	51	79	20
12	Slough Town	30	6	8	16	51	79	20
13	Dorking	30	7	6	17	54	91	20
14	Worthing	30	9	2	19	53	103	20
15	Wembley	30	7	5	18	49	86	19
16	Eastbourne	30	3	6	21	33	88	12

1961-62 Corinthian Football League

		P	W	D	L	F	A	Pts
1	Maidenhead United	30	23	3	4	77	31	49
2	**Chesham United**	**30**	**19**	**4**	**7**	**64**	**34**	**42**
3	Horsham	30	18	3	9	88	57	39
4	Edgware Town	30	15	7	8	47	40	37
5	Dagenham	30	16	3	11	65	49	35
6	Uxbridge	30	14	5	11	47	41	33
7	Erith & Belvedere	30	14	5	11	56	57	33
8	Slough Town	30	13	4	13	47	49	30
9	Wokingham Town	30	11	6	13	50	49	28
10	Leatherhead	30	10	7	13	63	52	27
11	Letchworth Town	30	8	9	13	55	65	25
12	Worthing	30	10	5	15	52	67	25
13	Eastbourne	30	8	6	16	39	57	22
14	Dorking	30	8	6	16	55	90	22
15	Epsom & Ewell	30	8	2	20	47	81	18
16	Wembley	30	7	2	21	40	73	16

1962-63 Corinthian Football League

		P	W	D	L	F	A	Pts
1	Leatherhead	30	22	5	3	88	36	49
2	Erith & Belvedere	30	18	6	6	61	32	42
3	Wokingham Town	30	18	5	7	53	41	41
4	Dagenham	30	15	8	7	64	47	38
5	Uxbridge	30	15	7	8	73	51	37
6	Letchworth Town	30	16	3	11	75	50	35
7	Maidenhead United	30	12	9	9	61	46	33
8	Slough Town	30	12	9	9	62	54	33
9	**Chesham United**	**30**	**11**	**6**	**13**	**66**	**59**	**28**
10	Worthing	30	12	4	14	63	78	28
11	Dorking	30	9	6	15	56	70	24
12	Horsham	30	10	3	17	50	74	23
13	Edgware	30	9	5	16	43	66	23
14	Eastbourne	30	7	5	18	43	76	19
15	Epsom & Ewell	30	5	5	20	31	82	15
16	Wembley	30	4	4	22	46	73	12

1962-63 Corinthian Football League Reserve Section

		P	W	D	L	F	A	Pts
1	Maidenhead United	30	24	4	2	93	35	52
2	Dagenham	30	22	2	6	91	34	46
3	Letchworth Town	30	20	4	6	98	39	44
4	**Chesham United**	**30**	**18**	**4**	**8**	**117**	**58**	**40**
5	Leatherhead	30	15	8	7	74	49	38
6	Erith & Belvedere	30	16	5	9	77	53	37
7	Uxbridge	30	13	6	11	55	53	32
8	Slough Town	30	12	5	13	65	58	29
9	Wokingham Town	30	12	4	14	63	73	28
10	Edgware Town	30	8	12	10	53	70	28
11	Eastbourne	30	9	3	18	58	79	21
12	Dorking	30	8	5	17	51	81	21
13	Worthing	30	7	6	17	61	87	20
14	Horsham	30	8	3	19	49	118	19
15	Wembley	30	5	5	20	36	82	15
16	Epsom	30	4	2	24	41	112	10

1963-64 Athenian Football League Division I Seniors

		P	W	D	L	F	A	Pts
1	Leatherhead	26	18	3	5	86	45	39
2	Worthing	26	18	2	6	76	40	38
3	Edgware Town	26	17	4	5	72	40	38
4	Erith & Belvedere	26	12	8	6	46	30	32
5	Slough Town	26	15	2	9	54	37	32
6	Letchworth Town	26	12	6	8	80	52	30
7	**Chesham United**	**26**	**14**	**2**	**10**	**75**	**57**	**30**
8	Uxbridge	26	11	5	10	45	42	27
9	Wokingham Town	26	11	3	12	42	54	25
10	Wembley	26	8	4	14	48	67	20
11	Eastbourne	26	7	3	16	44	75	17
12	Dorking	26	7	2	17	44	74	16
13	Horsham	26	4	3	19	27	67	11
14	Epsom & Ewell	26	4	1	21	45	104	9

1963-64 Athenian Football League Division I Reserves

		P	W	D	L	F	A	Pts
1	Letchworth Town	26	18	6	2	84	38	42
2	**Chesham United**	**26**	**17**	**1**	**8**	**61**	**46**	**35**
3	Wembley	26	14	5	7	64	51	33
4	Slough Town	26	12	7	7	70	42	31
5	Erith & Belvedere	26	13	5	8	66	43	31
6	Leatherhead	26	14	2	10	73	46	30
7	Wokingham Town	26	11	5	10	57	50	27
8	Edgware Town	26	9	9	8	49	54	27
9	Epsom & Ewell	26	9	5	12	60	64	23
10	Uxbridge	26	7	9	10	47	49	23
11	Worthing	26	9	1	16	53	65	19
12	Horsham	26	6	6	14	41	64	18
13	Eastbourne	26	7	3	16	33	73	17
14	Dorking	26	2	4	20	25	98	8

1964-65 Athenian Football League Division I

		P	W	D	L	F	A	Pts
1	Slough Town	30	21	6	3	81	23	48
2	Hemel Hempstead Town	30	21	4	5	77	32	46
3	**Chesham United**	**30**	**21**	**3**	**6**	**64**	**38**	**45**
4	Horsham	30	17	3	10	74	47	37
5	Harrow Town	30	16	5	9	79	56	37
6	Hertford Town	30	16	3	11	51	41	35
7	Letchworth Town	30	16	3	11	68	60	35
8	Erith & Belvedere	30	14	5	11	48	49	33
9	Tilbury	30	13	4	13	57	49	30
10	Eastbourne	30	9	9	12	53	67	27
11	Wokingham Town	30	8	6	16	50	63	22
12	Uxbridge	30	6	9	15	48	59	21
13	Harlow Town	30	6	6	18	37	66	18
14	Wembley	30	5	6	19	31	66	16
15	Dorking	30	5	5	20	31	92	15
16	Epsom & Ewell	30	6	3	21	52	93	13

Epsom & Ewell had two points deducted

1965-66 Athenian Football League Division I

		P	W	D	L	F	A	Pts
1	Bishops Stortford	30	24	3	3	84	33	51
2	Harwich & Parkeston	30	23	0	7	66	36	46
3	Hertford Town	30	17	7	6	58	26	41
4	Letchworth Town	30	17	7	6	80	49	41
5	Wembley	30	15	7	8	56	48	37
6	**Chesham United**	**30**	**15**	**4**	**11**	**74**	**52**	**34**
7	Erith & Belvedere	30	13	8	9	55	44	34
8	Redhill	30	16	0	14	56	44	32
9	Harlow Town	30	11	7	12	53	55	29
10	Tilbury	30	10	4	16	58	66	24
11	Dorking	30	11	1	18	50	75	23
12	Uxbridge	30	7	6	17	49	65	20
13	Wokingham Town	30	7	5	18	37	74	19
14	Harrow Town	30	7	5	18	32	71	19
15	Horsham	30	5	5	20	50	84	15
16	Eastbourne	30	6	3	21	45	81	15

1966-67 Athenian Football League Division I

		P	W	D	L	F	A	Pts
1	Hornchurch	30	20	6	4	51	24	46
2	Redhill	30	19	7	4	71	32	45
3	**Chesham United**	**30**	**17**	**5**	**8**	**57**	**34**	**35**
4	Wembley	30	15	5	10	49	40	35
5	Croydon Amateurs	30	17	0	13	71	48	34
6	Erith & Belvedere	30	12	6	12	54	41	30
7	Hertford Town	30	13	4	13	41	42	30
8	Letchworth Town	30	12	5	13	70	64	29
9	Harlow Town	30	10	8	12	39	42	28
10	Carshalton Athletic	30	11	6	13	43	49	28
11	Tilbury	30	11	5	14	63	64	27
12	Cheshunt	30	9	7	14	41	45	25
13	Dorking	30	10	5	15	42	60	25
14	Wokingham Town	30	10	3	17	47	66	23
15	Uxbridge	30	9	5	16	35	72	23
16	Harrow Borough	30	5	3	22	37	88	13

1967-68 Athenian Football League Division I

		P	W	D	L	F	A	Pts
1	Cheshunt	30	18	6	6	59	30	42
2	Wembley	30	16	8	6	67	37	40
3	Tilbury	30	16	6	8	58	35	38
4	Erith & Belvedere	30	14	9	7	55	41	37
5	Hertford Town	30	15	7	8	49	38	37
6	Croydon Amateurs	30	11	14	5	47	27	36
7	Carshalton Athletic	30	15	6	9	54	38	36
8	Dorking	30	13	6	11	37	31	32
9	Ware	30	12	6	12	42	49	30
10	Eastbourne United	30	11	6	13	44	47	28
11	**Chesham United**	**30**	**8**	**12**	**10**	**33**	**38**	**28**
12	Wokingham Town	30	11	5	14	53	70	27
13	Letchworth Town	30	11	3	16	50	52	25
14	Harlow Town	30	6	7	17	33	59	19
15	Worthing	30	6	5	19	35	58	17
16	Edgware Town	30	1	6	23	11	77	8

1968-69 Athenian Football League Division I Seniors

		P	W	D	L	F	A	Pts
1	Tilbury	30	20	5	5	65	28	45
2	Eastbourne United	30	19	6	5	70	40	44
3	Lewes	30	15	9	6	57	39	39
4	Hertford Town	30	16	6	8	48	28	38
5	Wokingham Town	30	12	11	7	44	28	35
6	Dorking	30	13	7	10	54	51	33
7	Erith & Belvedere	30	9	13	8	48	48	31
8	Carshalton Athletic	30	11	8	11	47	40	30
9	Harlow Town	30	12	4	14	47	49	28
10	Croydon Amateurs	30	7	12	11	39	45	26
11	Aylesbury United	30	8	10	12	45	64	26
12	**Chesham United**	**30**	**8**	**9**	**13**	**44**	**42**	**25**
13	Letchworth Town	30	8	8	14	41	56	24
14	Ware	30	8	6	16	44	69	22
15	Hemel Hempstead	30	6	6	18	32	67	18
16	Leyton	30	5	6	19	37	68	16

1969-70 Athenian Football League Division I Seniors

		P	W	D	L	F	A	Pts
1	Lewes	30	20	5	5	59	20	45
2	Boreham Wood	30	20	5	5	66	27	45
3	Erith & Belvedere	30	15	9	6	59	33	39
4	Aveley	30	16	5	9	65	44	37
5	Hertford Town	30	14	6	10	43	31	34
6	Harlow Town	30	15	4	11	53	47	34
7	**Chesham United**	**30**	**11**	**10**	**9**	**53**	**43**	**32**
8	Dorking	30	10	10	10	39	37	30
9	Carshalton Athletic	30	11	7	12	39	39	29
10	Hounslow	30	11	5	14	37	43	27
11	Aylesbury United	30	9	8	13	38	50	26
12	Hornchurch	30	8	9	13	30	36	25
13	Wokingham Town	30	9	7	14	34	51	25
14	Letchworth Town	30	8	5	17	41	74	21
15	Ware	30	4	9	17	35	81	17
16	Croydon Amateurs	30	5	4	21	28	63	14

1969-70 Athenian Football League Division I Reserves

		P	W	D	L	F	A	Pts
1	Boreham Wood	26	19	5	2	63	24	43
2	**Chesham United**	**26**	**20**	**2**	**4**	**77**	**28**	**42**
3	Hornchurch	26	17	5	4	55	26	39
4	Aylesbury United	26	14	6	6	51	36	34
5	Lewes	26	13	7	6	51	31	33
6	Croydon Amateurs	26	9	7	10	41	43	25
7	Erith & Belvedere	26	10	5	11	33	36	25
8	Aveley	26	10	5	11	38	42	25
9	Hounslow	26	11	2	13	46	50	24
10	Harlow Town	26	6	10	10	40	58	22
11	Hertford Town	26	6	8	12	48	50	20
12	Carshalton Athletic	26	8	4	14	41	46	20
13	Ware	26	5	10	11	33	58	20
14	Dorking	26	5	8	13	37	53	18
15	Letchworth Town	26	5	4	17	37	78	14
16	Wokingham Town	26	4	4	18	36	68	12

1970-71 Athenian Football League Division I Senior Section

		P	W	D	L	F	A	Pts
1	Aveley	30	18	8	4	59	24	44
2	Erith & Belvedere	30	19	6	5	67	34	44
3	Hornchurch	30	18	5	7	54	30	41
4	Horsham	30	16	6	8	62	36	38
5	Carshalton Athletic	30	15	6	9	51	35	36
6	Hertford Town	30	12	10	8	55	42	34
7	Wokingham Town	30	13	8	9	39	32	34
8	Edmonton	30	15	3	12	50	54	33
9	Dorking	30	11	9	10	36	40	31
10	Aylesbury United	30	11	7	12	45	47	29
11	Finchley	30	8	12	10	29	33	28
12	Harlow Town	30	6	9	15	35	54	21
13	**Chesham United**	**30**	**7**	**5**	**18**	**37**	**57**	**19**
14	Letchworth United	30	7	4	19	30	62	18
15	Eastbourne United	30	5	6	19	26	57	16
16	Hounslow	30	4	6	20	25	63	14

1970-71 Athenian Football League Reserve Section, Group Two-Autumn

		P	W	D	L	F	A	Pts
1	**Chesham United**	**14**	**10**	**3**	**1**	**45**	**14**	**23**
2	Aylesbury United	14	9	4	1	43	26	22
3	Finchley	14	8	2	4	31	23	18
4	Edmonton	14	5	3	6	31	34	13
5	Hertford Town	14	6	1	7	25	31	13
6	Harlow Town	14	5	1	8	26	34	11
7	Wokingham Town	14	4	1	9	31	39	9
8	Letchworth Town	14	0	3	11	17	48	3

1970-71 Athenian Football League Reserve Section, Group Two-Spring

		P	W	D	L	F	A	Pts
1	**Chesham United**	**14**	**8**	**5**	**1**	**31**	**11**	**21**
2	Finchley	14	8	2	4	24	12	18
3	Aylesbury United	14	6	1	7	26	27	13
4	Letchworth Town	14	5	3	6	20	24	13
5	Edmonton	14	4	5	5	17	21	13
6	Wokingham Town	14	4	4	6	24	24	12
7	Hertford Town	14	5	2	7	17	34	12
8	Harlow Town	14	2	6	6	17	23	10

1971-72 Athenian Football League Division I

		P	W	D	L	F	A	Pts
1	Harlow Town	30	22	5	3	96	40	49
2	Croydon Amateurs	30	20	6	4	77	25	46
3	Horsham	30	17	6	7	59	34	40
4	Carshalton Athletic	30	16	7	7	57	37	39
5	Marlow	30	12	11	7	53	41	35
6	Hertford Town	30	16	3	11	58	49	35
7	Finchley	30	12	9	9	43	43	33
8	**Chesham United**	**30**	**12**	**8**	**10**	**45**	**33**	**32**
9	Eastbourne United	30	10	8	12	48	51	28
10	Herne Bay	30	10	8	12	43	51	28
11	Dorking	30	10	6	14	48	62	26
12	Edmonton	30	9	7	14	47	61	25
13	Wokingham Town	30	7	6	17	30	51	20
14	Letchworth Town	30	5	6	19	34	61	16
15	Aylesbury United	30	4	8	18	42	90	16
16	Hounslow	30	3	6	21	33	84	12

1972-73 Athenian Football League Division I

		P	W	D	L	F	A	Pts
1	Horsham	30	24	3	3	74	24	51
2	Staines Town	30	20	3	7	54	32	43
3	Grays Athletic	30	16	5	9	33	27	37
4	Hounslow	30	13	7	10	49	36	33
5	Wokingham Town	30	11	7	12	51	47	29
6	Carshalton Athletic	30	11	7	12	41	42	29
7	Eastbourne United	30	11	7	12	32	38	29
8	Letchworth Town	30	10	9	11	32	43	29
9	Marlow	30	11	6	13	40	38	28
10	**Chesham United**	**30**	**11**	**5**	**14**	**41**	**41**	**27**
11	Edmonton	30	9	9	12	41	45	27
12	Finchley	30	10	6	14	43	46	26
13	Herne Bay	30	10	6	14	45	62	26
14	Worthing	30	7	10	13	29	42	24
15	Aylesbury United	30	8	6	16	38	58	22
16	Dorking	30	6	8	16	26	48	20

1973-74 Isthmian League Division II

		P	W	D	L	F	A	Pts
1	Dagenham	30	22	4	4	68	23	70
2	Slough Town	30	18	6	6	46	23	60
3	Hertford Town	30	17	5	8	46	29	56
4	**Chesham United**	**30**	**16**	**6**	**8**	**61**	**43**	**54**
5	Aveley	30	16	5	9	50	28	53
6	Tilbury	30	14	5	11	47	36	47
7	Maidenhead United	30	12	11	7	36	30	47
8	Horsham	30	12	9	9	47	35	45
9	Harwich & Parkeston	30	11	9	10	46	41	42
10	Staines Town	30	10	8	12	34	41	38
11	Carshalton Athletic	30	8	8	14	34	51	32
12	Hampton	30	6	10	14	33	51	28
13	Harlow Town	30	6	9	15	33	48	27
14	Finchley	30	6	7	17	29	52	25
15	Southhall	30	3	10	17	17	52	19
16	Wokingham Town	30	3	8	19	30	74	17

1974-75 Isthmian League Division II

		P	W	D	L	F	A	Pts
1	Staines Town	34	23	2	9	65	23	71
2	Southall	34	20	3	11	55	41	63
3	Tilbury	34	19	5	10	64	36	60
4	Harwich & Parkeston	34	18	4	12	52	44	58
5	**Chesham United**	**34**	**17**	**6**	**11**	**59**	**39**	**57**
6	St Albans City	34	15	11	8	42	37	56
7	Harlow Town	34	16	6	12	53	47	54
8	Horsham	34	16	5	13	59	49	53
9	Maidenhead United	34	13	7	14	38	40	46
10	Hampton	34	12	7	15	44	42	43
11	Croydon	34	11	10	13	48	55	43
12	Hertford Town	34	10	7	17	35	52	37
13	Boreham Wood	34	7	15	12	41	49	36
14	Wokingham Town	34	10	6	18	32	43	36
15	Finchley	34	9	9	16	36	53	36
16	Carshalton Athletic	34	9	9	16	38	58	36
17	Aveley	34	9	7	18	34	63	34
18	Corinthian Casuals	34	8	9	17	35	59	33

1975-76 Isthmian League Division II

		P	W	D	L	F	A	Pts
1	Tilbury	42	32	6	4	97	30	102
2	Croydon	42	28	14	0	81	27	98
3	Carshalton Athletic	42	28	6	8	75	37	90
4	**Chesham United**	**42**	**21**	**12**	**9**	**91**	**51**	**75**
5	Harwich & Parkeston	42	21	11	10	78	56	74
6	Hampton	42	21	9	12	72	52	72
7	St Albans City	42	18	12	12	59	48	66
8	Boreham Wood	42	17	12	13	68	50	63
9	Harrow Borough	42	15	12	15	71	74	57
10	Hornchurch	42	15	11	16	61	61	56
11	Horsham	42	14	13	15	60	55	55
12	Wembley	42	14	13	15	51	54	55
13	Wokingham Town	42	13	16	13	45	52	55
14	Walton & Hersham	42	14	12	16	61	56	54
15	Finchley	42	14	11	17	52	53	53
16	Bromley	42	11	11	20	64	86	44
17	Aveley	42	11	9	22	34	51	42
18	Harlow Town	42	11	9	22	50	73	42
19	Maidenhead United	42	6	17	19	32	65	35
20	Ware	42	7	12	23	50	95	33
21	Hertford Town	42	5	9	28	32	87	24
22	Corinthian Casuals	42	4	7	31	42	113	19

1976-77 Isthmian League Division II

		P	W	D	L	F	A	Pts
1	Boreham Wood	42	33	4	5	80	26	103
2	Carshalton Athletic	42	25	12	5	80	33	87
3	Harwich & Parkeston	42	23	8	11	93	61	77
4	Wembley	42	23	8	11	82	58	77
5	Harrow Borough	42	21	12	9	78	44	75
6	Horsham	42	23	5	14	67	56	74
7	Bromley	42	20	10	12	71	46	70
8	Oxford City	42	20	8	14	73	55	68
9	Hampton	42	20	8	14	62	45	68
10	Wokingham Town	42	16	14	12	60	44	62
11	Hornchurch	42	18	7	17	62	53	61
12	**Chesham United**	**42**	**17**	**10**	**15**	**63**	**66**	**61**
13	St Albans City	42	16	12	14	59	53	60
14	Walton & Hersham	42	17	9	16	57	56	60
15	Aveley	42	14	8	20	49	62	50
16	Corinthian Casuals	42	13	6	23	52	75	45
17	Harlow Town	42	11	8	23	39	77	41
18	Hertford Town	42	9	9	24	45	80	36
19	Maidenhead United	42	8	8	26	36	73	32
20	Clapton	42	7	9	28	43	87	30
21	Finchley	42	5	13	24	36	82	28
22	Ware	42	5	8	29	43	98	23

1977-78 Isthmian League Division I

		P	W	D	L	F	A	Pts
1	Dulwich Hamlet	42	28	9	5	91	25	93
2	Oxford City	42	26	5	11	85	44	83
3	Bromley	42	23	13	6	74	41	82
4	Walton & Hersham	42	22	11	9	69	41	77
5	Ilford	42	21	14	7	57	47	77
6	St Albans City	42	22	10	10	83	46	76
7	Wokingham Town	42	19	12	11	68	48	69
8	Harlow Town	42	19	8	15	63	49	65
9	Harrow Borough	42	17	10	15	59	54	61
10	Maidenhead United	42	16	13	13	55	54	61
11	Hertford Town	42	15	14	13	57	51	59
12	**Chesham United**	**42**	**14**	**13**	**15**	**69**	**70**	**55**
13	Hampton	42	13	13	16	49	53	52
14	Harwich & Parkeston	42	12	13	17	68	79	49
15	Wembley	42	15	3	24	56	82	48
16	Horsham	42	12	10	20	41	57	46
17	Finchley	42	11	13	18	41	68	46
18	Aveley	42	13	7	22	47	75	46
19	Ware	42	8	13	21	61	95	37
20	Clapton	42	10	6	26	46	78	36
21	Hornchurch	42	8	10	24	47	81	34
22	Corinthian Casuals	42	3	10	29	40	88	19

1978-79 Isthmian League Division I

		P	W	D	L	F	A	Pts
1	Harlow Town	42	31	7	4	93	32	100
2	Harrow Borough	42	26	8	8	85	49	86
3	Maidenhead United	42	25	6	11	72	50	81
4	Bishop's Stortford	42	22	11	9	68	40	77
5	Horsham	42	23	7	12	63	47	76
6	Hertford Town	42	21	11	10	62	41	74
7	Harwich & Parkeston	42	22	5	15	90	57	71
8	Bromley	42	18	12	12	76	50	66
9	Epsom & Ewell	42	18	7	17	69	57	61
10	Wembley	42	15	14	13	57	50	59
11	Aveley	42	17	6	19	57	67	57
12*	Wokingham Town	42	17	8	17	64	68	56
13	Clapton	42	15	8	19	67	80	53
14	Metropolitan Police	42	12	13	17	58	55	49
15	Walton & Hersham	42	12	9	21	47	71	45
16	Ilford	42	13	5	24	48	80	44
17	Ware	42	11	10	21	46	69	43
18	**Chesham United**	**42**	**11**	**9**	**22**	**46**	**66**	**42**
19	Finchley	42	7	15	20	43	74	36
20	St Albans City	42	7	7	28	43	90	28
21	Southall & Ealing Boro	42	5	5	32	41	114	20

* Three points deducted

1979-80 Isthmian League Division I

		P	W	D	L	F	A	Pts
1	Leytonstone & Ilford	42	31	6	5	83	35	99
2	Bromley	42	24	10	8	93	44	82
3	Maidenhead United	42	24	8	10	81	46	80
4	Bishop's Stortford	42	24	8	10	74	47	80
5	Kingstonian	42	22	8	12	59	44	74
6	**Chesham United**	**42**	**18**	**13**	**11**	**68**	**56**	**67**
7	St Albans City	42	17	13	12	65	47	64
8	Farnborough Town	42	19	7	16	70	57	64
9	Epsom & Ewell	42	18	7	17	62	57	61
10	Camberley Town	42	16	10	16	43	38	58
11	Walton & Hersham	42	15	12	15	61	50	57
12	Wembley	42	16	8	18	46	52	56
13	Wokingham Town	42	14	11	17	45	49	53
14	Hertford Town	42	13	11	18	71	74	50
15	Aveley	42	12	13	17	45	55	49
16	Hampton	42	14	7	21	57	74	49
17	Finchley	42	13	9	20	44	59	48
18	Metropolitan Police	42	13	8	21	46	67	47
19	Ware	42	11	12	19	45	61	45
20	Clapton	42	14	3	25	48	77	45
21*	Harwich & Parkeston	42	11	6	25	51	84	38
22	Horsham	42	6	4	32	29	113	22

* 1 point deducted

1980-81 Isthmian League Division I

		P	W	D	L	F	A	Pts
1	Bishop's Stortford	42	30	6	6	84	28	96
2	Billericay Town	42	29	6	7	67	34	93
3	Epsom & Ewell	42	24	12	6	80	36	34
4	Farnborough Town	42	23	11	8	75	39	80
5	St Albans City	42	24	5	13	85	61	77
6*	Kingstonian	42	20	9	13	63	52	66
7	Oxford City	42	18	9	15	71	48	63
8	Wokingham Town	42	16	15	11	70	56	63
9	Metropolitan Police	42	18	7	17	61	58	61
10	**Chesham United**	**42**	**17**	**7**	**18**	**64**	**64**	**58**
11	Lewes	42	17	7	18	72	83	58
12	Maidenhead United	42	16	7	19	58	62	55
13	Walton & Hersham	42	12	15	15	46	53	51
14	Hertford Town	42	13	11	18	46	65	50
15	Hampton	42	12	13	17	46	53	49
16	Aveley	42	13	9	20	54	55	48
17	Wembley	42	13	8	21	47	61	47
18	Clapton	42	12	8	22	53	86	44
19	Ware	42	9	13	20	50	69	40
20*	Tilbury	42	10	8	24	42	84	35
21	Camberley Town	42	8	7	27	42	88	31
22	Finchley	42	6	11	25	36	77	29

* 3 points deducted

1981-82 Isthmian League Division I

		P	W	D	L	F	A	Pts
1	Wokingham Town	40	29	5	6	86	30	92
2	Bognor Regis Town	40	23	10	7	65	34	79
3	Metropolitan Police	40	22	11	7	75	48	77
4	Oxford City	40	21	11	8	82	47	74
5	Feltham	40	20	8	12	65	49	68
6	Lewes	40	19	7	14	73	66	64
7	Hertford Town	40	16	10	14	62	54	58
8	Wembley	40	14	15	11	69	55	57
9	Farnborough Town	40	15	11	14	71	57	56
10	Epsom & Ewell	40	16	8	16	52	44	56
11	Kingstonian	40	16	7	17	57	56	55
12	Hampton	40	15	9	16	52	52	54
13	Hornchurch	40	13	15	12	42	50	54
14	Aveley	40	14	10	16	46	58	54
15	St Albans City	40	14	9	17	55	55	51
16	Maidenhead United	40	11	10	19	49	70	43
17	Tilbury	40	9	15	16	49	66	42
18	Walton & Hersham	40	10	11	19	43	65	41
19	**Chesham United**	**40**	**9**	**9**	**22**	**41**	**71**	**36**
20	Clapton	40	9	7	24	44	75	34
21	Ware	40	5	2	33	29	105	17

1982-83 Isthmian League Division I

		P	W	D	L	F	A	Pts
1	Worthing	40	25	6	9	76	39	81
2	Harlow Town	40	21	11	8	84	55	74
3	Farnborough Town	40	20	13	7	69	39	73
4	Hertford Town	40	20	11	9	70	61	71
5	Oxford City	40	19	13	8	70	49	70
6	Boreham Wood	40	21	6	13	62	42	69
7	Metropolitan Police	40	19	9	12	77	57	69
8	Walton & Hersham	40	17	6	17	65	59	57
9	Hampton	40	15	10	15	62	60	55
10	Wembley	40	14	10	16	62	61	52
11	Aveley	40	15	7	18	52	62	52
12	Kingstonian	40	13	12	15	53	53	51
13	Tilbury	40	12	10	18	41	47	46
14	Feltham	40	11	12	17	45	54	45
15	**Chesham United**	**40**	**13**	**6**	**21**	**43**	**70**	**45**
16	Epsom & Ewell	40	10	14	16	44	49	44
17	Lewes	40	12	8	20	47	71	44
18	Cheshunt	40	10	13	17	41	49	43
19	Hornchurch	40	11	8	21	45	74	41
20	Maidenhead United	40	10	10	20	57	87	40
21	*St Albans City	40	10	9	21	52	79	37

* 2 points deducted

1983-84 Isthmian League Division I

		P	W	D	L	F	A	Pts
1	Farnborough Town	42	26	8	8	101	45	86
2	Kingstonian	42	23	10	9	67	39	79
3**	Leatherhead	42	23	10	9	109	61	76
4	**Chesham United**	**42**	**22**	**8**	**12**	**78**	**46**	**74**
5	Wembley	42	20	10	12	59	40	70
6	St Albans City	42	19	10	13	79	60	67
7	Tilbury	42	18	13	11	86	68	67
8	Bromley	42	18	9	15	71	64	63
9	Hampton	42	17	11	14	75	62	62
10	Staines Town	42	16	11	15	59	53	59
11	Maidenhead United	42	17	8	17	65	64	59
12*	Walton & Hersham	42	16	8	18	60	69	55
13	Aveley	42	16	7	19	62	78	55
14	Oxford City	42	14	12	16	62	53	54
15	Lewes	42	15	9	18	70	72	54
16	Basildon United	42	15	8	19	55	61	53
17	Boreham Wood	42	15	7	20	72	83	52
18	Hornchurch	42	15	6	21	55	74	51
19	Woking	42	15	6	21	60	91	51
20	Metropolitan Police	42	10	12	20	65	92	42
21	Clapton	42	5	11	26	50	124	26
22	Hertford Town	42	5	10	27	36	97	25

* 1 point deducted ** 3 points deducted

1984-85 Isthmian League Division I

		P	W	D	L	F	A	Pts
1	Windsor & Eton	42	26	7	9	89	44	85
2	Epsom & Ewell	42	23	9	10	73	51	78
3	Wembley	42	21	11	10	65	32	74
4	Maidenhead United	42	22	8	12	67	42	74
5	Boreham Wood	42	22	7	13	74	43	73
6	Farnborough Town	42	18	12	12	78	60	66
7	Hampton	42	18	12	12	65	49	66
8	Metropolitan Police	42	20	5	17	79	64	65
9	**Chesham United**	**42**	**18**	**8**	**16**	**64**	**57**	**62**
10	Tilbury	42	17	10	15	54	64	61
11	Leatherhead	42	15	10	17	67	56	55
12	Aveley	42	15	10	17	49	53	55
13	Woking	42	16	7	19	66	73	55
14	Hertford Town	42	15	9	18	56	73	54
15	Oxford City	42	14	9	19	57	56	51
16	Lewes	42	13	12	17	49	65	51
17	Walton & Hersham	42	13	10	19	52	70	49
18	Hornchurch	42	13	10	19	43	63	49
19	Kingstonian	42	13	9	20	47	67	48
20	Clapton	42	12	11	19	49	67	47
21	Cheshunt	42	12	8	22	45	64	44
22	Feltham	42	7	4	31	31	106	25

1985-86 Isthmian League Division I

		P	W	D	L	F	A	Pts
1	St Albans City	42	23	11	8	92	61	80
2	Bromley	42	24	8	10	68	41	80
3	Wembley	42	22	12	8	59	30	78
4	Oxford City	42	22	11	9	75	51	77
5	Hampton	42	21	11	10	63	45	74
6	Leyton-Wingate	42	21	10	11	77	56	73
7	Uxbridge	42	20	8	14	64	49	68
8	Staines Town	42	18	10	14	69	66	64
9	Boreham Wood	42	15	16	11	62	54	61
10	Walton & Hersham	42	16	10	16	68	71	58
11	Lewes	42	16	8	18	61	75	56
12	Leytonstone-Ilford	42	13	15	14	57	67	54
13	Finchley	42	12	17	13	61	59	53
14	Grays Athletic	42	13	11	18	69	75	50
15	Leatherhead	42	14	8	20	62	68	50
16	Tilbury	42	13	11	18	60	66	50
17	Maidenhead United	42	13	7	22	61	67	46
18	Basildon United	42	12	9	21	52	72	45
19	Hornchurch	42	11	11	20	44	59	44
20	**Chesham United**	**42**	**12**	**6**	**24**	**51**	**87**	**42**
21	Harlow Town	42	8	14	20	53	70	38
22	Aveley	42	8	6	28	59	98	30

1986-87 Isthmian League Division II North

		P	W	D	L	F	A	Pts
1	**Chesham United**	**42**	**28**	**6**	**8**	**81**	**48**	**90**
2	Wolverton Town	42	23	14	5	74	32	83
3	Haringey Borough	42	22	13	7	86	40	79
4	Heybridge Swifts	42	21	11	10	81	54	74
5	Aveley	42	19	13	10	68	50	70
6	Letchworth Gdn City	42	19	11	12	77	62	68
7	Barton Rovers	42	18	11	13	49	39	65
8	Tring Town	42	19	7	16	69	49	64
9	Collier Row	42	19	5	18	67	65	62
10	Ware	42	17	8	17	51	50	59
11	Saffron Walden Town	42	14	14	14	56	54	56
12	Wivenhoe Town	42	15	11	16	61	61	56
13	Vauxhall Motors	42	15	10	17	61	57	55
14	Hornchurch	42	13	16	13	60	60	55
15	Hertford Town	42	14	13	15	52	53	55
16	Berkhamsted Town	42	12	16	14	62	64	52
17	Harlow Town	42	13	11	18	45	55	50
18	Rainham Town	42	12	11	19	53	70	47
19	Clapton	42	10	11	21	45	63	41
20	Hemel Hempstead	42	10	11	21	45	63	41
21	Royston Town	42	4	12	26	37	109	24
22	Cheshunt	42	5	6	31	43	114	21

1987-88 Isthmian League Division I

		P	W	D	L	F	A	Pts
1	Marlow	42	32	5	5	100	44	101
2	Grays Athletic	42	30	10	2	74	25	100
3	Woking	42	25	7	10	91	52	82
4	Boreham Wood	42	21	9	12	65	45	72
5	Staines Town	42	19	11	12	71	48	68
6	Wembley	42	18	11	13	54	46	65
7	Basildon United	42	18	9	15	65	58	63
8	Walton & Hersham	42	15	16	11	53	44	61
9	Hampton	42	17	10	15	59	54	61
10	Leatherhead	42	16	11	15	64	53	59
11	Southwick	42	13	12	17	59	63	51
12	Oxford City	42	13	12	17	70	77	51
13	Worthing	42	14	8	20	67	73	50
14	Kingsbury Town	42	11	17	14	62	69	50
15	Walthamstow Avenue	42	13	11	18	53	63	50
16	Lewes	42	12	13	17	83	77	49
17	Uxbridge	42	11	16	15	41	47	49
18	**Chesham United**	**42**	**12**	**10**	**20**	**69**	**77**	**46**
19	Bracknell Town	42	12	9	21	54	80	45
20	Billericay Town	42	11	11	20	58	88	44
21	Stevenage Borough	42	11	9	22	36	64	42
22	Wolverton Town	42	3	3	36	23	124	12

1988-89 Isthmian League Division I

		P	W	D	L	F	A	Pts
1	Staines Town	40	26	9	5	79	29	87
2	Basingstoke Town	40	25	8	7	85	36	83
3	Woking	40	24	10	6	72	30	82
4	Hitchin Town	40	21	11	8	60	32	74
5	Wivenhoe Town	40	22	6	12	62	44	72
6	Lewes	40	21	8	11	72	54	71
7	Walton & Hersham	40	21	7	12	56	36	70
8	Kingsbury Town	40	20	7	13	65	41	67
9	Uxbridge	40	19	7	14	60	54	64
10	Wembley	40	18	6	16	45	58	60
11	Boreham Wood	40	16	9	15	57	52	57
12	Leatherhead	40	14	8	18	56	58	50
13	Metropolitan Police	40	13	9	18	52	68	48
14	**Chesham United**	**40**	**12**	**9**	**19**	**54**	**67**	**45**
15	Southwick	40	9	15	16	44	58	42
16	Chalfont St Peter	40	11	9	20	56	82	42
17	Hampton	40	7	14	19	37	62	35
18*	Worthing	40	8	10	22	49	80	32
19	Collier Row	40	8	7	25	37	82	31
20	Bracknell Town	40	8	6	26	38	70	30
21	Basildon United	40	6	7	27	34	77	25

1989-90 Isthmian League Division I

		P	W	D	L	F	A	Pts
1	Wivenhoe Town	42	31	7	4	94	36	100
2	Woking	42	30	8	4	102	29	98
3	Southwick	42	23	15	4	68	30	84
4	Hitchin Town	42	22	13	7	60	30	79
5	Walton & Hersham	42	20	10	12	68	50	70
6	Dorking	42	19	12	11	66	41	69
7	Boreham Wood	42	17	13	12	60	59	64
8	Harlow Town	42	16	13	13	60	53	61
9	Metropolitan Police	42	16	11	15	54	59	59
10	**Chesham United**	**42**	**15**	**12**	**15**	**46**	**49**	**57**
11	Chalfont St Peter	42	14	13	15	50	59	55
12	Tooting & Mitchum	42	14	13	15	42	51	55
13	Worthing	42	15	8	19	56	63	53
14	Whyteleafe	42	11	16	15	50	65	49
15	Lewes	42	12	11	19	55	65	47
16	Wembley	42	11	10	21	57	68	43
17	Croydon	42	9	16	17	43	57	43
18	Uxbridge	42	11	10	21	52	75	43
19	Hampton	42	8	13	21	28	51	37
20	Leatherhead	42	7	10	25	34	77	31
21	Purfleet	42	7	8	27	33	78	29
22*	Kingsbury Town	42	8	10	24	45	78	25

* Nine points deducted

1990-91 Isthmian League Division I

		P	W	D	L	F	A	Pts
1	**Chesham United**	**42**	**27**	**8**	**7**	**102**	**37**	**89**
2	Bromley	42	22	14	6	62	37	80
3	Yeading	42	23	8	11	75	45	77
4	Aveley	42	21	9	12	76	43	72
5	Hitchin Town	42	21	9	12	78	50	72
6	Tooting & Mitcham Utd	42	20	12	10	71	48	72
7	Walton & Hersham	42	21	8	13	73	48	71
8	Molesey	42	22	5	15	65	46	71
9	Whyteleafe	42	21	6	15	62	53	69
10	Dorking	42	20	5	17	78	67	65
11	Chalfont St Peter	42	19	5	18	56	63	62
12	Dulwich Hamlet	42	16	11	15	67	54	59
13	Harlow Town	42	17	8	17	73	64	59
14	Boreham Wood	42	15	8	19	46	53	53
15	Wembley	42	13	12	17	62	59	51
16	Uxbridge	42	15	5	22	45	61	50
17	Croydon	42	15	5	22	44	85	50
18	Heybridge Swifts	42	13	10	19	46	59	49
19	Southwick	42	13	8	21	49	75	47
20	Lewes	42	10	8	24	49	82	38
21	Metropolitan Police	42	9	6	27	55	76	33
22	Worthing	42	2	4	36	28	157	10

1991-92 Diadora League Premier Division

		P	W	D	L	F	A	Pts
1	Woking	42	30	7	5	96	25	97
2	Enfield	42	24	7	11	59	45	79
3	Sutton United	42	19	13	10	88	51	70
4	**Chesham United**	**42**	**20**	**10**	**12**	**67**	**48**	**70**
5	Wokingham Town	42	19	10	13	73	58	67
6	Marlow	42	20	7	15	56	50	67
7	Aylesbury United	42	16	17	9	69	46	65
8	Carshalton Athletic	42	18	8	16	64	67	62
9	Dagenham	42	15	16	11	70	59	61
10	Kingstonian	42	17	8	17	71	65	59
11	Windsor & Eton	42	15	11	16	56	56	56
12	Bromley	42	14	12	16	51	57	54
13	St Albans City	42	14	11	17	66	70	53
14	Basingstoke Town	42	14	11	17	56	65	53
15	Grays Athletic	42	14	11	17	53	68	53
16	Wivenhoe Town	42	16	4	22	56	81	52
17	Hendon	42	13	9	20	59	73	48
18	Harrow Borough	42	11	13	18	58	78	46
19	Hayes	42	10	14	18	52	63	44
20	Staines Town	42	11	10	21	43	73	43
21	Bognor Regis Town	42	9	11	22	51	89	38
22	Bishop's Stortford	42	7	12	23	41	68	33

1992-93 Diadora League Premier Division

		P	W	D	L	F	A	Pts
1	**Chesham United**	**42**	**30**	**8**	**4**	**104**	**34**	**98**
2	St Albans City	42	28	9	5	103	50	93
3	Enfield	42	25	6	11	94	48	81
4	Carshalton Athletic	42	22	10	10	96	56	76
5	Sutton United	42	18	14	10	74	57	68
6	Grays Athletic	42	18	11	13	61	64	65
7	Stevenage Borough	42	18	8	16	62	60	62
8	Harrow Borough	42	16	14	12	59	60	62
9	Hayes	42	16	13	13	64	59	61
10	Aylesbury United	42	18	6	18	70	77	60
11	Hendon	42	12	18	12	52	54	54
12	Basingstoke Town	42	12	17	13	49	45	53
13	Kingstonian	42	14	10	18	59	58	52
14	Dulwich Hamlet	42	12	14	16	52	66	50
15	Marlow	42	12	11	19	72	73	47
16	Wokingham Town	42	11	13	18	62	81	46
17	Bromley	42	11	13	18	51	72	46
18	Wivenhoe	42	13	7	22	41	75	46
19	Yeading	42	11	12	19	58	66	45
20	Staines Town	42	10	13	19	59	77	43
21	Windsor & Eton	42	8	7	27	40	90	31
22	Bognor Regis	42	5	10	27	46	106	25

1993-94 Diadora League Premier Division

		P	W	D	L	F	A	Pts
1	Stevenage Borough	42	31	4	7	88	39	97
2	Enfield	42	28	8	6	80	28	92
3	Marlow	42	25	7	10	90	67	82
4	**Chesham United**	**42**	**24**	**8**	**10**	**73**	**45**	**80**
5	Sutton United	42	23	10	9	77	31	79
6	Carshalton Athletic	42	22	7	13	81	53	73
7	St Albans City	42	21	10	11	81	54	73
8	Hitchin Town	42	21	7	14	81	56	70
9	Harrow Borough	42	18	11	13	54	56	65
10	Kingstonian	42	18	9	15	101	64	63
11	Hendon	42	18	9	15	61	51	63
12	Aylesbury United	42	17	7	18	64	67	58
13	Hayes	42	15	8	19	63	72	53
14	Grays Athletic	42	15	5	22	56	69	50
15	Bromley	42	14	7	21	56	69	49
16	Dulwich Hamlet	42	13	8	21	52	74	47
17	Yeading	42	11	13	18	58	66	46
18	Molesey	42	11	11	20	44	62	44
19	Wokingham Town	42	11	6	25	38	67	39
20	Dorking	42	9	4	29	58	104	31
21	Basingstoke Town	42	5	12	25	38	86	27
22	Wivenhoe Town	42	5	3	34	38	152	18

1994-95 Diadora League Premier Division

		P	W	D	L	F	A	Pts
1	Enfield	42	26	9	5	106	43	93
2	Slough Town	42	22	13	7	82	56	79
3	Hayes	42	20	14	8	66	47	74
4	Aylesbury United	42	21	6	15	86	59	69
5	Hitchin Town	42	18	12	12	68	59	66
6	Bromley	42	18	11	13	76	67	65
7	St Albans City	42	17	13	12	96	81	64
8	Molesey	42	18	8	16	65	61	62
9	Yeading	42	14	15	13	60	59	57
10	Harrow Borough	42	17	6	19	64	67	57
11	Dulwich Hamlet	42	16	9	17	70	82	57
12	Carshalton Athletic	42	16	9	17	69	84	57
13	Kingstonian	42	16	8	18	62	57	56
14	Walton & Hersham	42	14	11	17	75	73	53
15	Sutton United	42	13	12	17	74	69	51
16	Purfleet	42	13	12	17	76	90	51
17	Hendon	42	12	14	16	54	65	50
18	Grays Athletic	42	11	16	15	57	61	49
19	Bishop's Stortford	42	12	11	19	53	76	47
20	**Chesham United**	**42**	**12**	**9**	**21**	**60**	**86**	**45**
21	Marlow	42	10	9	23	52	84	39
22	Wokingham Town	42	6	9	27	39	86	27

1995-96 ICIS League Division I

		P	W	D	L	F	A	Pts
1	Oxford City	42	28	7	7	98	60	91
2	Heybridge Swifts	42	27	7	8	97	43	88
3	Staines Town	42	23	11	8	82	59	80
4	Leyton Pennant	42	22	7	13	73	57	73
5	Aldershot Town	42	21	9	12	81	46	72
6	Billericay Town	42	19	9	14	58	58	66
7	Bognor Regis Town	42	18	11	13	71	53	65
8	Marlow	42	19	5	18	72	75	62
9	Basingstoke Town	42	16	13	13	70	60	61
10	Uxbridge	42	16	12	14	46	49	60
11	Wokingham Town	42	16	10	16	62	65	58
12	**Chesham United**	**42**	**15**	**12**	**15**	**51**	**44**	**57**
13	Thame United	42	14	13	15	64	73	55
14	Maidenhead United	42	12	14	16	50	63	50
15	Whyteleafe	42	12	13	17	71	81	49
16	Abingdon	42	13	9	20	63	80	48
17	Barton Rovers	42	12	10	20	69	87	46
18	Berkhamsted Town	42	11	11	20	52	68	44
19	Tooting & Mitcham	42	11	10	21	45	64	43
20	Ruislip Manor	42	11	9	22	55	77	42
21	Wembley	42	11	8	23	49	66	41
22	Barking	42	4	12	26	35	90	24

1996-97 ICIS League Division I

		P	W	D	L	F	A	Pts
1	**Chesham United**	**42**	**27**	**6**	**9**	**80**	**46**	**87**
2	Basingstoke Town	42	22	13	7	81	38	79
3	Walton & Hersham	42	21	13	8	67	41	76
4	Hampton	42	21	12	9	62	39	75
5	Billericay Town	42	21	12	9	69	49	75
6	Bognor Regis Town	42	21	9	12	63	44	72
7	Aldershot Town	42	19	14	9	67	45	71
8	Uxbridge	42	15	17	10	65	48	62
9	Whyteleafe	42	18	7	17	71	68	61
10	Molesey	42	17	9	16	50	53	60
11	Abingdon Town	42	15	11	16	44	42	56
12	Leyton Pennant	42	14	12	16	71	72	54
13*	Maidenhead United	42	15	10	17	57	57	52
14	Wokingham Town	42	14	10	18	41	45	52
15	Thame United	42	13	10	19	57	69	49
16	Worthing	42	11	11	20	58	77	44
17	Barton Rovers	42	11	11	20	31	58	44
18	Croydon	42	11	10	21	40	57	43
19	Berkhamsted Town	42	11	9	22	47	66	42
20	Canvey Island	42	9	14	19	52	71	41
21	Marlow	42	11	6	25	41	84	39
22	Tooting & Mitcham	42	8	8	26	40	85	32

Managers of Chesham United

F Hayes	1919
E Coughtrey	1921
J Humphrey	
S Ringsell	

For the intervening period the Club team was picked by a Club committee.
In 1949 the Club's first paid manager was appointed.

W Bott	1949 - 53
T Beeson	1953 - 57
J Baynham	1957 - 66
S Prosser	1966 - 67
J Reardon	1967 - 69
B Darvill	1969 - 70
B McNally	1970 - 79
M Hall	1979 - 81
M Taylor	1981 - 82
L Craker	1982 - 83
P Morrissey	1984 - 85
G Martin	1985
D Russell	1985 - 86
B Gould	1986 - 87
J Delaney	1987 - 88
J Pratt	1988
P Morrissey	1988
A Taylor	1988
J Clements	1988 - 90
G Borg	1990 - 91
G Aplin	1991 - 94
A Randall	1994
P Roberts	1994 - 95
J Kelman	1995 - 96
P O'Reily	1996
A Thomas	1996 - 97
S Emmanuel	1997 -98
G. Roberts	1998 - date

Programmes through the Years

*Published every Saturday during the Season by
The Carlton Press, Broadway, Chesham.*

Chesham United

FOOTBALL CLUB.

OFFICIAL PROGRAMME

Price One Penny.

SATURDAY, OCTOBER 1st, 1921,

VERSUS

SEER GREEN

BUCKS CHARITY CUP (Junior).

Kick-off 3.30 p.m.

Chesham United v. Seer Green
Bucks Charity Cup 1921

*Published every Saturday during the Season
by The Carlton Press, Broadway, Chesham.* 852

CHESHAM UNITED

FOOTBALL CLUB.

Season 1921-2.—Champions: Spartan League, Divs. I. & II;
Chesham League, Div. I.
Winners: Berks & Bucks Senior Cup; Bucks Senior
Charity Cup; and Chesham Challenge Cup.

OFFICIAL PROGRAMME

No. 29.]   *Price One Penny.*

MONDAY, APRIL 2nd, 1923.

VERSUS

WEALDSTONE

SPARTAN LEAGUE (Div. I).

Kick-off 3.30 o'clock.

Chesham United v. Wealdstone
Spartan League Div. I, 1923

Programmes through the Years

WATCH THIS NO. 520

Chesham United Football Club

OFFICIAL PROGRAMME · · 1d.

Hon. Sec.—Mr. J. G. STONE.   Treasurer—Mr. F. J. WILSON, 60 The Broadway.   Bankers—LLOYDS LIMITED.

1921 - 22.—Champions :
Spartan League, Divs.
I. and II. ; Chesham
League, Div. I.
Winners: Berks & Bucks
Senior Cup ; Bucks
Senior Charity Cup ;
& Chesham Challenge
Cup.

1922-23. — Champions :
Spartan League, Div. I.
Winners : Bucks Senior
Charity Cup ; Apsley
Senior Charity Cup.

No. 1.   SEPT. 15th, 1923.

Chesham United Second Eleven (Champions, 1921-22).

THE CENTRE POSITION for reliable MEN'S WEAR is
opposite the POST OFFICE. Just call in after the Match
and inspect our READY-TO-WEAR STOCK. Deliveries of
WINTER UNDERWEAR constantly arriving.

DON'T PUT IT OFF ! BUT PUT IT ON !

S. BAKER, Gentlemen's Outfitter

E. J. BALDWIN,

Tobacconist and Newsagent,

8, Red Lion Street, Chesham.

Best value in Pipes, Pouches, Cigarette Cases
and Tubes.

Chesham United v Marlow
Bucks Charity Cup, 1923

Programmes through the Years

OFFICIAL PROGRAMME, 1d.   WATCH THIS NO.

No. 2.   SEPTEMBER 26th, 1925.

Chesham United Football Club

Headquarters—SPORTS GROUND, NEW ROAD, CHESHAM.

1921-22.—Champions : Spartan League, Divs. I. and II. ; Chesham League, Div. I. Winners : Berks & Bucks Senior Cup; Bucks Senior Charity Cup; and Chesham Challenge Cup.   1922-23.—Champions : Spartan League, Div. I. Winners: Bucks Senior Charity Cup; and Apsley Senior Charity Cup.   1923-24.—Winners : Chesham and District Charity Cup.
1924-25.—Champions : Spartan League, Div. I. Winners: Bucks Senior Charity Cup ; Aylesbury Hospital Cup ; Berks & Bucks Junior Cup.

Hon. Sec.—   Hon. Treas.—   Bankers—
Mr. J. G. STONE.   Mr. F. J. WILSON, 60, The Broadway.   LLOYDS BANK LTD.

INSURANCE.—*Agents for all the principal Companies. Expert advice given free.*
TRAVEL.—*Rail Tickets issued in advance.*   *Passages Booked to any part of the world. Tours arranged, Home or abroad.*
AIR TRAVEL.—*Agents for Imperial Airways, Ltd.*   **MORTGAGES** *arranged.*

Call,
Write or
Phone—

BUCKS INSURANCE BUREAU, LTD.,

Insurance Brokers and Travel Agents,

Town Hall, CHESHAM, — *and* — Oakfield Corner, AMERSHAM,
Phone 119.   *Managing Director,* CLARENCE D. DEFRIEZ, A.C.I.B.   Phone 77.

A Separate Department has now been opened for **DUPLICATING & TYPEWRITING.**
Concert Programmes, Price Lists, etc.   Circulars from 3/6 per 100.

The "GEORGE" Commercial Hotel
Chesham

LUNCHEONS :: TEAS :: DINNERS
CATERING A SPECIALITY.

Choice Wines, Spirits and Cigars

Telephone No. 141 (Chesham).   T. S. COLLINS, *Proprietor.*

Chesham United v Wendover
Bucks Charity Cup, 1925

Programmes through the Years

Chesham United v. Waterlows,
Spartan League Premier Division 1933

Programmes through the Years

Chesham United v. Hastings
Corinthian League, 1947

Chesham United v. Hastings
Berks & Bucks Senior Cup, 1948

Programmes through the Years

Chesham United v. Maidenhead Utd
Corinthian League, 1952

Chesham United v All Stars
George Robinson's Benefit Match, 1960

The cover of Chesham United's Handbook, 1958

Programmes through the Years

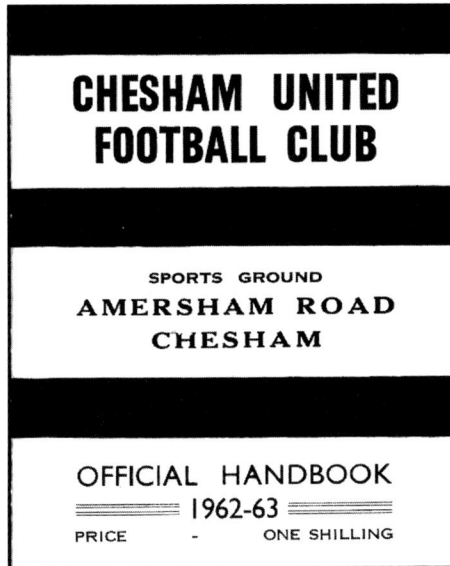

CHESHAM UNITED FOOTBALL CLUB

SPORTS GROUND
AMERSHAM ROAD
CHESHAM

OFFICIAL HANDBOOK
1962-63
PRICE - ONE SHILLING

Chesham United's 1962 Handbook

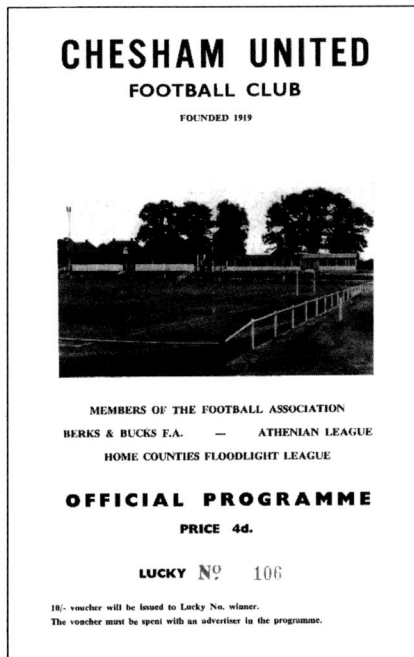

CHESHAM UNITED
FOOTBALL CLUB
FOUNDED 1919

MEMBERS OF THE FOOTBALL ASSOCIATION
BERKS & BUCKS F.A. — ATHENIAN LEAGUE
HOME COUNTIES FLOODLIGHT LEAGUE

OFFICIAL PROGRAMME
PRICE 4d.

LUCKY Nº 106

10/- voucher will be issued to Lucky No. winner.
The voucher must be spent with an advertiser in the programme.

Chesham United v. Harrow
Athenian League Div 1, 1966

Programmes through the Years

CHESHAM UNITED
Football Club

AMERSHAM ROAD, CHESHAM, BUCKS.

Chesham 2456

MEMBERS OF THE FOOTBALL ASSOCIATION

BERKS & BUCKS F.A.   ROTHMANS ISTHMIAN LEAGUE

MIDDLESEX BORDER LEAGUE   MITHRAS CUP

PREMIER MID—WEEK FLOODLIT LEAGUE

AMATEUR CUP FINALISTS 1968

OFFICIAL   PROGRAMME

PRICE   SEASON 1973/4

all
the
LOCAL
SPORTS
NEWS

IN
THE
BUCKS
EXAMINER

EVERY FRIDAY

price 4p

CHESHAM UNITED HONOURS
FOUNDED 1st DECEMBER 1917.

BERKS & BUCKS F.A. COUNTY CUP WINNERS
SENIOR CUP   JUNIOR CUP
1922, 1926, 1929, 1934,   1925, 1928,
1948, 1951, 1965, 1967.   1932, 1948.

SPARTAN LEAGUE 1919/1947   CORINTHIAN LEAGUE 1947/63
Winners Div. One   Memorial Shield Winners
1922, 1923, 1925.   1961, 1963.
Premier Division   Neale Trophy Winners
1933.   1963.
Division Two (Reserves)
1921.   MIDDLESEX BORDER LGE. 1972/
                                    Winners 1972

ATHENIAN LEAGUE 1963/73
Memorial Shield Winners 1964, 1965.
Neale Trophy Winner 1964.

Chesham United v Maidenhead
1st Round of Amateur Cup, 1973

Programmes through the Years

Programme for the 3rd Round FA Cup game
against Cambridge United, 1980

Chesham United v Hampton
Isthmian League, 1983

Chesham United v Walton & Hersham
Isthmian League Division 1 1981

Programme for the Berks & Bucks Cup
Final 1985 played at Maidenhead

Programmes through the Years

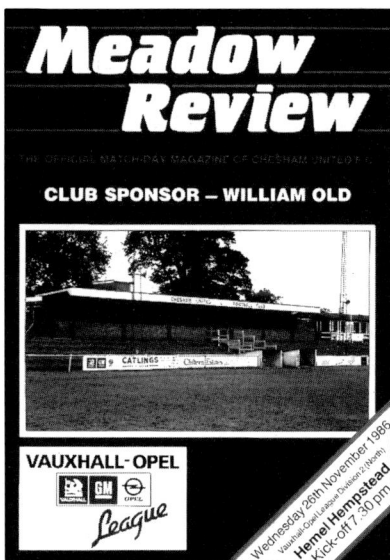

Chesham United v Hemel Hempstead
Vauxhall-Opel League Div 2 North 1986
Chesham won the title this season

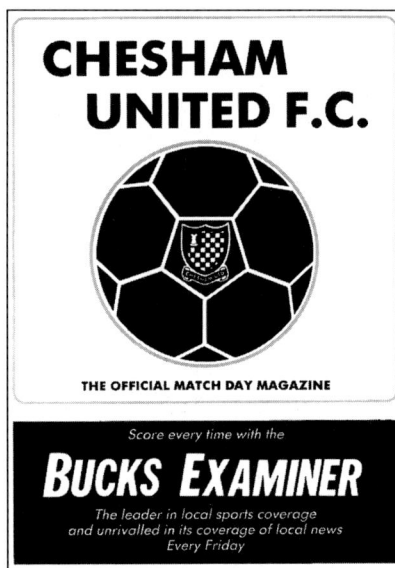

Chesham United v. Hampton 1985
Isthmian League Division 1

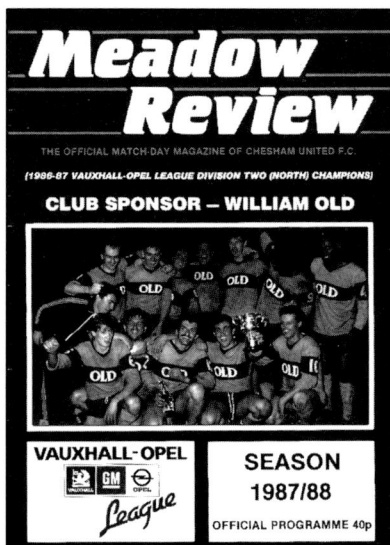

Chesham United v Walton & Hersham
Vauxhall-Opel League Div 1 1987
The cover shows the 1986 championship side

Programmes through the Years

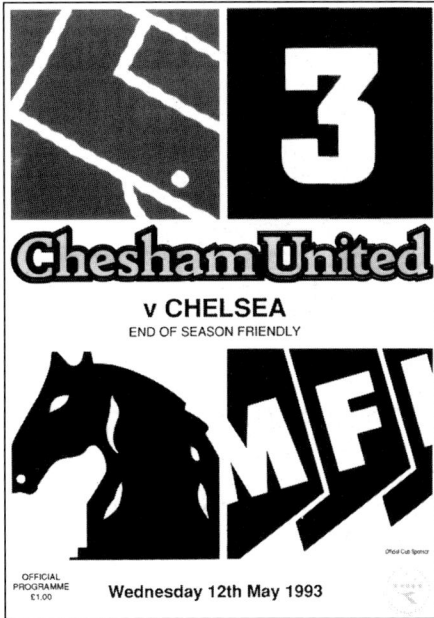

*Programme for the match against
First Division Chelsea,
End-of-season friendly 1993*

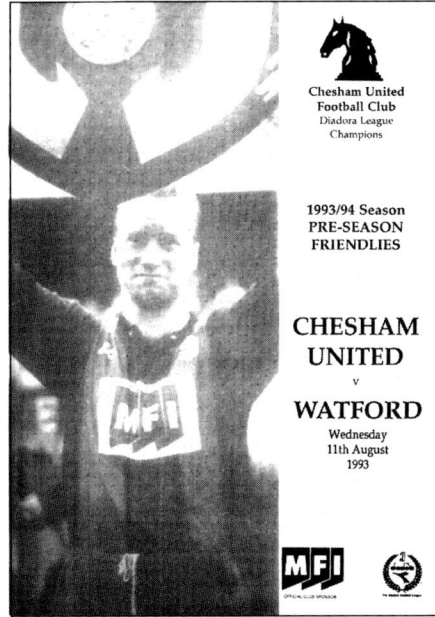

*Pre-season friendly:
Chesham United v. Watford, 1993*

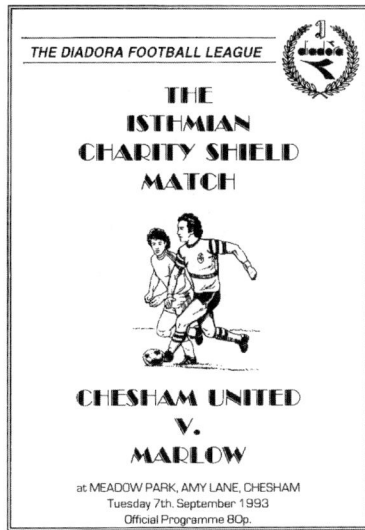

*Charity Shield Match v Marlow
September 1993*

Programmes through the Years

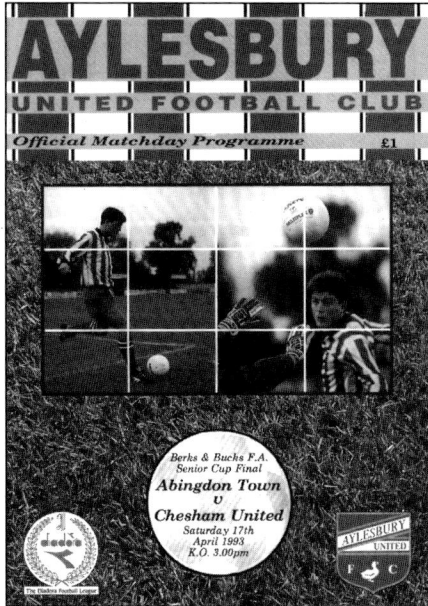

Away programme for
Berks & Bucks Cup Final 1993
Abingdon Town v Chesham United
Played at Aylesbury

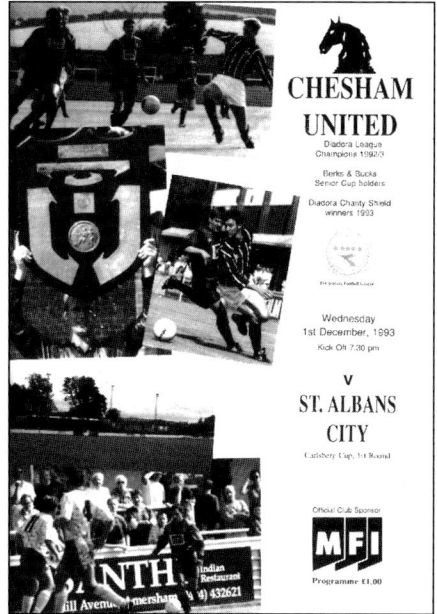

Carlsberg Cup 1993
Chesham United v St Albans City

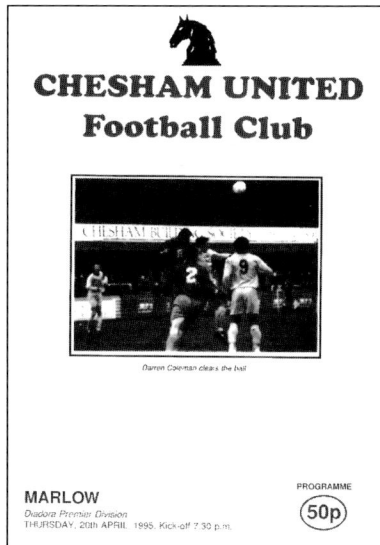

Diadora Premier Division 1995 v Marlow